GENERAL SCIENCE AND TECHNOLOGY FOR BPSC

BEST BOOK FOR CONCEPT BUILDING

ADITYA RAJ ANAND

I want to dedicate this book to my self and my journey of life and my love towards physics and chemistry. When I was 18, Sciencelaws.in plays a biggest role in my life. Sciencelaws.in is a science and information blog run by the author Mrs. Aditya Raj Anand. Here you get all the updates regarding science and technology.

Even I have written many of the blog post on science and technology. If you want to read then you can follow us on sciencelaws.in website as well as sciencelaws.in instagram account.

Contents

FOREWORD

Author Aditya Raj Anand

Why Author Write this book. Author Believes that science can be understant if it is expressed in easy language. That is the biggest reason to write this book.

One more interesting think about the Author Mrs. Aditya Raj Anand is that he was studying, he also felt the problems to understand science. Because science can be understood if it is expressed in easy language.

So, he decided language will not make the problem to understand science for anyone more.

This book is written for those who has a weak basics on physics and chemsistry.

PREFACE

Our Other UseFul Books.

Physics for class 9 Available on Amazon Kindle only

Available on amazon, flipkar

This book is also Available on Amazon. Just type Physics class 9 by Aditya Raj Anand, You will get all the books that is written by me.

Prologue

Hello, My name is Aditya Raj Anand an author, digital marketer, blogger, and an entrepreneur. You can follow me on instagram @sciencelaws.in

Follow Sciencelaws.in website for more updates on physics, chemistry and mathematics.

At Science Laws website you can ask questions in our question community and discuss the science as well.

I

UNIT AND MEASUREMENT

Unit of Measurement and time

Physics:- The study of nature and natural things.

1. It is the made of greek word " Fusis" means natural things and nature.
2. It means that physics is the study of nature and its laws.
3. Physics is the foundation of engineering and technology.
4. Physics is based in experiment when experiments are done then it measure with the help of physical quantity.
5. Quantity means it represents the number.

Physical quantity

- It is represent of the physical laws in the term id quantity.

It is of two types

1. Scalar quantity and
2. vector quantity.

- Scalar quantity means it has only magnitude not direction.
- vector quantity means it has both magnitude and as well as direction.

Units

It is of two types

1. Fundamental unit
2. Derived unit

- Fundamental unit:- It is not depend another unit, three fundamental unit are mass, length and Time.
- Derived unit:- It is depend in fundamental unit.

system of unit are four types

1. Mks system:- In this system Length, Mass and Time are expressed in meter, Kilogram, and Second.
2. Fps system:- In this system Length, Mass and Time is expressed in Foot, Pound, second.
3. CGs system:- In this system Length, Mass and Time is expressed in Centimeter, Gram, second.
4. S.I system;- (international System of Unit) In S.I system having seven fundamental unit.

30 physical quantities with their si units and cgs units

Here is a collection of 30 fundamental and derived physical quantities which commonly used in physics with their si units and CGS units. Also describe the derived quantity with derivation.

We have already discussed about the definition of physical quantity in the above definition. But lets define the physical quantity in another words.

Physical quantity are those quantities which represents the quantities of any material with the help of some symbols attached with numerical values. For example a container contains 6 kilograms of wheat. So we can write 6 kg. Here kg is the physical quantity attached with numerical value of 6.

As we have already seen above that, Physical quantities are two types first is fundamental quantity and second is derived quantity. These are the following 30 physical quantities (both fundamental and derived) with their si units and CGS units. Before we start discussing following 30 physical quantities. Please note that some quantities are derived from fundamental quantity.

30 physical quantities with their si units and cgs units

(1.) Mass (M)
(2.) Distance (S)
(3.) Time (T)
(4.) Speed (s)
(5.) Volume (V)
(6.) Density (D)
(7.) Pressure (P)
(8.) Work (W)
(9.) Energy (E)
(10.) Electric current (A)
(11.) Velocity (V)
(12.) Acceleration (A)
(13.) Displacement (S)
(14.) Force (F)
(15.) torque (τ)
(16.) Electric field (E)
(17.) Angular velocity (ω)
(18.) Linear momentum (P)
(19.) Magnetic dipolc moment (?)
(20.) Thrust (T)
(21.) Temperature (T)
(22.) Frequency (μ)

(23.) Amount of substance (Mol)
(24.) Concentration (C)
(25.) Power (P)
(26.) Impulse (I)
(27.) Angle (∠)
(28.) Weight (W)
(29.) Magnetic field (B)
(30.) Gravitation (G)

Lets discuss all of these physical quantities with their definition along with their si and cgs unit.

(1.) Mass (M)

- Mass is the scale of measurement of inertia of any body or matter. mass represent the quantity that a body have. greater the mass of a body, less in impact of force in it. mass do not depends on shape and size of a body. that means the greater size of a body need not have a greater mass or vice-versa.
- S.I unit of mass:- Kilogram (Kg)
- CGS unit of mass:- Gram (g)

(2.) Distance (S)

- The actual path covered by the body during the whole journey. It is denoted by S. distance is different from displacement. both have some differences between them. Distance may be in straight line, curved line, or zigzag line. Distance can never be zero untill or unless the body is at rest.
- S.I unit of distance:- Meter (m)
- CGS unit of distance:- Centimetre (cm)

(3.) Time (T)

- Time is an illusion that loses in every second. time is an infinite unfinished continuous events that exist in present, fall in past and will next in future. time is denoted by t.
- S.I unit of time:- Second (s)
- CGS unit of time:- second (s)

(4.) Speed (s)

- Speed is define as the total distance travelled by the body to the total time taken. In other words speed is determined by the distance covered in a specific time period by the body. It is denoted by s.
- S.I unit of speed:- meter / sec (m/s)
- CGS unit of speed:- centimetre / sec (cm/s)

(5.) Volume (V)

- The maximum dimensional area covered by an object in length, breath and height. It is denoted by V. volume is affected by shape and size of a body. means if the body has greater shape and size it may be the body has larger volume or vice-versa.
- S.I unit of volume:- meter cube (m3)
- CGS unit of volume:- centimetre cube (cm3)

(6.) Density (D)

- Density is define as the mass of a body per unit volume. That means if a body has volume 'v' and mass 'm' then density is equal to m/v.
- S.I unit density:- kilogram / m2 (kg/m3)
- CGS unit density:- gram / cm3 (g /cm3)

(7.) Pressure (P)

- Pressure is the force exerted in a unit area of an object. It is denoted by P. pressure is also define as the force per unit area. given by P = F / A.
- S.I unit of pressure:- Newton / m2 (N / m2) or Pascal
- CGS unit pressure:- Dyne / cm2

(8.) Work (W)

- In physics, If a force is applied on a body and the body get displaces from its initial position and covers some distance then work is done. It is denoted by W. work can also be described as the dot product of force and displacement. given by W = F.s.
- S.I unit of work:- Joule (N-m) or Newton-meter.

- CGS unit of work:- Erg (dyne-cm) or Dyne-centimetre

(9.) Energy (E)

- The ability to do some work is called energy. energy can neither be created nor be destroyed but it can be converted into one form to another form. like electric energy into light energy. It is denoted by E.
- S.I unit of energy:- Joule
- CGS unit of energy:- Erg

(10.) Electric current (A)

- It is the flow of electron from one potential to another potential. Flow of electron create potential difference between two points so that electricity generated. It is denoted by A.
- S.I unit of electric current:- Ampere
- CGS unit of electric current:- Biot

(11.) Velocity (V)

Velocity is define as the distance travelled by the body per unit time in a given direction. Velocity is vector quantity. because it has both magnitude and direction. It is denoted by V. velocity can also be described as the displacement per unit time.

Velocity = Displacement / time

S.I unit of velocity:- meter / sec. (m /s)

CGS unit of velocity:- centimetre / sec. (cm /s)

(12.) Acceleration (A)

Acceleration is the change in velocity with respect to time. In other words, it is the final displacement minus initial displacement whole divided by time. It is denoted by A. Acceleration is vector quantity.

S.I unit of acceleration:- meter / sec2 (m / s2)

CGS unit of acceleration:- centimetre / sec2 (cm / s2)

(13.) Displacement (S)

It is the shortest distance covered by the body in whole journey. In other words, displacement is equal to the distance between initial position and final position of a body. It is denoted by S. Distance may be zero.

S.I unit of displacement:- meter (m)

CGS unit of displacement:- centimetre (cm)

(14.) Force (F)

Force is define as the push or pull of an object is called force. In other words, force is the product of mass and acceleration. It is denoted by F. where F = ma.

S.I unit of force:- Newton (Kg. m /s2)

CGS unit of force:- Dyne (g. cm /s2)

(15.) torque (τ)

It is the measurement of the force acting on a body to determine how much it cause to rotate the body. It is denoted by τ. It is vector quantity.

S.I unit of torque:- Newton-meter (N-m)

CGS unit of torque:- Dyne-centimetre

(16.) Electric field (E)

It is a reason where electric current can be experienced. In other words, electric field is the area where the electric field lines exist. It is denoted by E.

S.I unit of electric field:- Newton / coulomb (volt / meter)

CGS unit of electric field:- Dyne / biot-sec.

(17.) Angular velocity (ω)

Rate of change of angular displacement with respect to time. On other hand angular velocity is how fast the body is moving with respect to time.

S.I unit of angular velocity:- radian / sec

CGS unit of angular velocity:- per second

(18.) Linear momentum (P)

Linear momentum is defined as the product of mass and velocity. It is denoted by P. yhe formula of linear momentum is P = mv. It is vector quantity.

S.I unit of liner momentum:- Kg. m /s

CGS unit of linear momentum:- g. cm /s

(19.) Magnetic dipole moment (?)

Magnetic dipole moment represent the magnetic strength of the magnet with the help of quantity. It is denoted by ?. It is vector quantity because it has both magnitude and direction.

S.I unit of magnetic dipole moment:- weber-meter

CGS unit of magnetic dipole moment:- emu. erg/G

(20.) Thrust (T)

Thrust is the types of force act on upward direction in water.

S.I unit of thrust:- Newton

CGS unit of thrust:- Dyne

(21.) Temperature (T)

It is define as the how hotness and coldness of the body is. It is denoted by T. In other words temperature indicates that how hot or cold a body is.

S.I unit of temperature:- kelvin (k)

CGS unit of temperature:- kelvin

(22.) Frequency (μ)

It is number of cycle of a wave passing in one second. In other words it is cycle per second.

S.I unit of frequency:- Hertz (Hz)

CGS unit of frequency:- Hertz

(23.) Amount of substance (Mol)

Amount of substance is defined as the total number of soute present in total number of solvent.

S.I unit of amount of substance:- Mole

CGS unit of amount of substance:- mole

(24.) Concentration (C)

Concentration is define as the total number of solute or solvent present in a unit volume of solution. In other words it calculate the mass of solute or solvent per unit volume. It is denoted by C.

S.I unit of concentration:- kilogram / m3

CGS unit of concentration:- gram / cm3

(25.) Power (P)

The rate of doing work is called power. power is work per unit time. It is denoted by P.

S.I unit of power:- joule / sec (watt)

CGS unit of power:- erg / sec

(26.) Impulse (I)

Impulse is the force acting for a short period of time.

S.I unit of Impulse:- Newton-second

CGS unit of Impulse:- Dyne-second

(27.) Angle (∠)

It is unitless that expressed in terms of theta.

(28.) Weight (W)

Weight is the force acting in downward direction to the center of the earth. It is the downward force.

S.I unit of weight:- Newton

CGS unit of weight:- Dyne

(29.) Magnetic field (B)

It is the reason where magnetic force is experienced. It is denoted by B.

S.I unit:- Tesla

CGS unit:- oersted

(30.) Gravitation (G)

It the pulling force acting in downward direction toward the center of the planet.

S.I unit:- Newton / kg

CGS unit:- Dyne / g

here you find the actual meaning of scalar and vector quantity. If we define scalar and vector quantity in simple word we can say that scalar quantity are those which have only magnitude not direction, but vector quantity are those which have both magnitude as well as direction. difference between scalar and vector quantity are given below the page for better understanding of these quantities.

There are many topics covered in this articles like,

What is scalar and vector quantity?

List of scalar and vector quantities and their units.

Difference between scalar and vector quantity.

Product of scalar and vector quantity.

What is scalar and vector field?

20 examples of scalar and vector quantity.

characteristics of scalar and vector quantities.

Types of vector.

vector addition and subtraction.

What is scalar and vector quantity?

What is scalar and vector quantity?

scalar quantity:- Those quantity which has only magnitude not direction are called scalar quantity.

for example length, mass, speed, work, density, volume etc.

lets understand by taking examples If we say the body have 10 kg of mass it doesn't means not 10 kg of mass in north or south direction.

In other words Those quantity which has only one dimension described by single element like one constant and one variable. for example 5m, 6cm, 2kg, 4mm etc,

Vector quantity:- Those quantity which has both magnitude and a specific direction are called vector quantity.

for example Displacement, Force, acceleration, velocity, torque, momentum etc.

lets understand by taking examples, suppose 2N of force act on the body in North direction, A body is accelerating 5m/s2 in upward direction, Weight (W= mg) of a body acted in the downward direction.

In other word Those quantity which has both two dimension and three dimension described by some more elements like 5m North, 3m/s2, 6m/s, 5N, etc.

List of scalar and vector quantities and their units.

- Mass
- kilogram(kg)

- Displacement
- meter(m)
- Distance
- Meter(m)

- Velocity
- m/s

- Time
- Second(s)

- Acceleration
- m/s2

- Speed
- m/s

- Force
- Newton(N)

- Volume
- m3

- Torque
- Newton meter(N-m)

- Density
- kg/m3

- Electric field
- volt per meter(v/m)

- Pressure
- Newton(N)

- Angular velocity
- radians per second

- Work
- Joule(J)

- Linear momentum
- kilogram meters per second(kg m/s)

- Energy
- Joule(J)

- Magnetic dipole moment
- Ampere meter(A-m)

- Electric current
- Ampere(A)

- Thrust
- Force(F)

20 examples of scalar and vector quantity.

- Mass

- Distance
- Time
- Speed
- Volume
- Density
- Pressure
- Work
- Energy
- Electric Current
- Length
- Refractive Index
- Area
- Power
- Heat
- Temperature
- Size
- Calories
- Frequency
- Cost
- 20 examples of vector quantities
- Displacement
- Velocity
- Torque
- Thrust
- Force
- Acceleration
- Electric field
- Angular momentum
- Angular velocity
- Drift velocity
- Magnetic dipole moment
- Linear momentum
- Average velocity
- Magnetic field
- Weight
- Gravitational force
- vector potential
- Poynting vector

- current density
- Magnetisation

Difference between scalar and vector quantity.

These are some differential points on scalars and vectors.

Scalar quantity:-

Scalar quantity has only magnitude.

They change if their magnitude change.

They can be added according to ordinary laws of algebra.

Vector quantity:-

vectors have both magnitude and direction

They change if either their magnitude, direction or both change.

They can be added only by using special laws of vector addition.

Product of scalar and vector quantity

Scalar product and vector product are the two different ways of multiplying two vectors. Multiplication of scalar product has its own rule and Multiplication of vectors product has its own way.

Scalar product (or dot product) of two vectors:- The scalar or dot product of two vectors A and B is defined as the product of the magnitudes of vectors A and B and cosine of the angle θ between them.

vector product (or cross product) of two vectors:- The vector or cross product of two vectors is defined as the vector whose magnitude is equal to the product of the magnitudes of two vectors and sine of the angle between them and whose direction is perpendicular to the plane of the two vectors.

What is scalar and vector field?

A scalar field is something that has a particular value at every point in space. for example temperature at every point on the earth has a particular value but if we move to and fro from that point then the value of temperature will change.

A vector field is just similar to scalar field because vector field also having a value at every point on space. but it has a value and direction at every point in space.

characteristics of scalar and vector quantities.

Before knowing the characteristic of scalar and vector quantities. we have to know he meaning of characteristic.

characteristic means a quality of something that makes him/her/it different from other people or thing.

so here characteristic of scalar and vector quantity has little same that is magnitude. lets understand it in more detailed.

characteristic of scalar quantities:- scalar quantity has only magnitude. there is no need of direction. speed, distance, time, temperature these all do not need direction.

for example Ramesh played for 3 hours. here we do not need direction.

characteristic of vector quantities:- vector quantities has also magnitude but it needs direction for their illustration. displacement, velocity, acceleration, force etc acquires direction.

for example a body start moving by 3m/s in forward direction. here direction included for better illustration.

Types of vector.

Position vector:- A vector which gives position of an object with reference to the origin of a co-ordinate system is called position vector.

Displacement vector:- It is that vector which tells how much and in which direction and object has changed its position in a given time interval.

Polar vector:- The vector which has a starting point or a point of application are called polar vector.

Axial vector:- The vector which represent rotational effect and act along the axis of rotation in right hand screw rule are called axial vector.

Equal vector:- Two vectors are said to be equal if they have the same magnitude and same direction.

Negative of a vector:- The negative of a vector is defined as another vector having the same magnitude but having an opposite direction.

Modulus of vector:- The modulus of a vector means the length or the magnitude of that vector.

Unit vector:- A unit vector is a vector of unit magnitude drawn in the direction of a given vector.

Fixed vector:- The vector whose initial point is fixed is called a fixed vector.

Zero vector:- a zero vector or null vector is a vector that has zero magnitude and an unknown direction.

vector addition and subtraction.

Two vectors can be added or can be subtracted by their rules and laws. vectors can be added by two famous laws

Triangle law of vector addition:- If two vectors can be represented both in magnitude and direction by the two sides of triangle taken in the same order, then their resultant is represented completely, both in magnitude and direction, by the third side of the triangle taken in the opposite order.

Parallelogram law of vector addition:- If two vectors can be represented both in magnitude and direction by the two adjacent sides of a parallelogram drawn from a common point, then their resultant is completely represented, both in magnitude and direction, by the diagonal of the parallelogram passing through the point. see the above picture for more illustration.

Please note that the same rules and theory also use in subtraction of two vectors but you have to replace plus sign from the minus sign.

FAQ on scalar and vector quantities

What is scalar and vector quantities?

scalar quantities are those quantities which has only magnitude not direction. speed, time, distance etc.

vector quantities are those quantities which has both magnitude and a specific direction. displacement, velocity, acceleration etc.

Is work scalar or vector?

work is scalar quantity which has only magnitude. w= f.s work is dot product of force and displacement. and we know that dot product is scalar quantity

can a scalar be negative?

Yes scalar can be negative. but it depends on situation and types of quantities. like temperature can be negative which is a scalar quantity.

Is force a scalar quantity?

No force is a vector quantity. because it has cross product of mass and acceleration. F= m✖?a cosθ.

Where do we use vectors?

vectors can be used in physics to represent physical quantities with direction in the upper head by arrow sign. it is used to represent displacement, velocity, acceleration, etc.

Can you square a vector?

No we cannot square a vector because a vector has both magnitude and direction. we can square its magnitude but not direction.

--------------- Team Science laws ---------------

II

Motion

Motion

In physics a things which can see, touch and feel is called object or body.

It is the branch of physics which deals with the study of the object at rest and in motion

Object in rest

A body is said to be rest if it does not change its position with respect to its surrounding with the passage of time.

Object in motion

If the position of the body changes its state with respect to its surrounding then body is called in motion.

Rest and motion are relative terms

Rest and motion are relative terms because object can be at rest with respect to one things and in motion with respect to some other things at the same time, so motion is not absolute, it is relative. for example---

Suppose you are sitting in a train which is moving then we are at rest with respect to the other passenger sitting in that compartment but in motion with respect to the objects on the ground.

Our house is at rest with respect to the other house on the earth but it is in motion with respect to an observer on the moon.

Types of motion

One dimension, two dimension motion, three dimension motion.

One dimension motion:-

The motion in a straight lines is called one - dimension motion.

Moving of bus in a straight line.

Falling of an apple from tree.

If only co - ordinate is used from three co - ordinate x, y and z then the motion is one dimension motion.

Two dimension motion;-

Motion in a plane is called two dimension motion.

If only two co - ordinate is used from three co - ordinate x, y and z then it is called two dimension.

The motion of object in horizontal and vertical circle.

The earth revolving around the sun.

S carom coin in motion.

Three dimension motion;-

Motion in space is called three dimension motion.

If all co - ordinate is used then it is called three dimension motion.

Position:-

If particles on the origin then its position will be zero.

If particles move along the positive direction of x - axis then its position positive.

If particles moves in the negative direction of x – axis then the position is negative.

Distance:-

The actual length of the path covered by an object is called distance.

The length of the actual path between the initial and final position of the body is called the distance.

Distance has no sense of direction hence distance is a scalar quantity.

It's S.I unit is 'm' .

Distance can never be negative.

Displacement:-

The shortest distance between two points is called displacement.

If the body moves in any direction then displacement is change in position.

If the initial and final position of the body are same then the displacement will be Zero.

Hence, from above result we can say that displacement will be positive, Negative or zero.

Displacement has sense of direction therefore displacement is a vector quantity.

S.I unit of displacement is 'm' .

It is not depend on path but distance is depend on path.

Distance is equal to displacement when it goes to straight line.

If we move on the straight lines in positive direction then distance is equal to the displacement but we move in curved path then distance is greater than displacement.

Uniform and non uniform motion

Uniform motion:- When a body moves in such a way that it covers equal distance in equal interval of time however small the time interval may be then speed is said to be uniform motion.

Non uniform motion:- if body travels equal distance in unequal interval of time/ unequal distance cover in equal interval of time then it is called non uniform motion.

What is Speed?

The distance traveled by a body per unit time over a short interval of time is called its speed.

S.I unit of speed is m/s.

C.Gs unit of speed is cm/s.
speed is the scalar quantity.

What is Velocity?

The displacement covered by a body per unit time is called velocity.
S.I unit of velocity is m/s.
C.Gs unit is cm/s.
velocity is vector quantity it has both magnitude and direction.

What is Average speed?

It is the ratio of total distance traveled by total time taken.
It is a scalar quantity.
It's S.I unit is m/s.
It is denoted by 'V' .

Wha is Acceleration?

Rate of change of velocity with respect to time.
Acceleration = final velocity - initial velocity/ time
a = v - u / t
S.I unit of acceleration is m/s2.
Acceleration may be positive, Negative or Zero.

Acceleration are two types

1. Uniform Acceleration:-

When a body travels in a straight lines and its velocity changes by equal amounts is equal interval of time then it is called Uniform acceleration.

2. Non uniform Acceleration:-

When the velocity of a body changes by unequal amount in equal interval of time then it is called non uniform acceleration.
Positive acceleration is simply called acceleration.
Negative acceleration is simply called Retardation.

Three equation of motion

1. First equation of motion
V = u + at
Proof :- we know that
acceleration = change in velocity/ time taken
a = v - u/t
at = v - u
at + u = v
or
v = u + at
Where,
V = final velocity
U = initial velocity
T = time
A = acceleration
2. Second equation of motion
S = ut + 1/2 at2
Proof
Average speed = u + v/2
Distance = Average speed * time
S =(u + v/2)* t
We know that
v = u + at
put value of v
S = ut + ut + at2/ 2
= 2 ut + at^2/ 2
S = ut + 1/2 at2
3. Third equation of motion
v2 – u2 + 2as
We know that,
V = u + at
and ,
S = ut + 1/2 at2
From V = u + at
t = v - u/a
S = ut + 1/2 at2
S = u*(v -u/a) + 1/2 * a *(v -u/a)2

2as + u2 = v2

v2 = u2 + 2as

------------- Team Science laws --------------

III

Force and Laws of Motion

Force and Laws of Motion

Force :- It may be defined as push or pull which produces (tends to produces) a change in the state of rest or uniform motion of a body or change in the direction of motion of the body.

Force may also change the Shape of the body or produces rotational effect.

Force is a vector quantity because Force have as well as magnitude and direction.

The non-living body also exert a Force.

Example:- (i) When we suspended a heavy block From a rope. The rope holds the block just as a man can hold in the air.

(ii) When a cork is dipped in Water it comes to the surface due to the upward. Force exerted by water.

Galileo's Experiment: (Aristotle)

(iii) When we comb our der hair and bring the comb close to bits of paper the piece jumps to the comb therefore, we can say the Force is interaction between two bodies.

A Greek philosopher give the idea that a constant Force is needed to keep a body moving with constant velocity it means that if a constant Force not applied the body will come to rest. Thus, the natural state of a body is that of rest.

In 17th century Galileo Galilei and Italian scientist opposed the idea of Aristotle according to Galileo no Force was needed to keep a body in constant velocity it means that natural state of a body it is oppose the change in its of motion.

Newton's 1st law of motion

Every object continuous in a state of rest or of uniform motion in a straight line if external force no applied on the body.

'Inertia' this term is well known for those who take interest in physics. Inertia is a very important part of physics. But our question is from where this inertia came. So a quite simple answer would be from "Newton's laws of motion". So in this post we will not only discuss the types of inertia and their examples but also we will try to find out how inertia originated from Newton's law.

A famous person said that there are total 10% physics covered if you know Newton's laws. Here Newton's laws means not only three laws but all the portions including inertia, momentum, etc.

Now, let's focus on our main topic that is inertia of rest. So before we start the definition of Inertia. Let's understand what we have to know to understand full concept of inertia of rest.

So these are the things and terms related to inertia that everyone should know to clear the full concept of inertia of rest.

What is inertia?
Types of inertia?
What is inertia of rest?
Inertia of rest in terms of Newton's law.
Deep discussion on inertia of rest.
Property of inertia of rest.
Factors depends on inertia of rest.
One experiment to demonstrate inertia of rest.
8 most common examples of inertia of rest in our daily life.

What is inertia?

We have studied in our previous classes that inertia is the tendency of a body to remain it in their original state. No matter whether the body is moving or stop.

In more simple way we can say that inertia is the legacy or identity of any object. Means that inertia indicates or tells about the nature of a body. But is that's it about inertia? Is there this limited information available about inertia?

We can't say anything because in our childhood we have just studied that much. So it's time to know more about inertia.

Apart from the types of inertia that we will discuss later in this post. Let's take a deep breath and lost on the deep analysis of inertia.

Everything in this universe is in two forms whether it may be in position of rest or in motion. Those bodies which are in a state of raised in this universe may because of some universal force or gravity. And those bodies which are in a state of motion may because of the some same universal force of gravity.

So how we can say that there has the body's tendency to remains at in state of rest or in state of motion. If something is in a state of rest may be because some force act on it. For example let's suppose a football is placed in playground. Now here two situation arises.

Situation No 1 :-

The football on the ground is at in a state of rest may because no one applied an external force on it.

Situation No 2 :-

The football on the ground is at in state of rest may because of the flat surface with gravity pulling. If the ground will be incline it will start moving with gravity force.

No from the above discussion on two situation. We have understood that inertia of anybody it is not only sustainable with external force. But also unbalanced force.

Hence, in the definition of inertia we have to say that inertia is the tendency of a body to remains its state of rest or uniform motion until or unless no any external or unbalanced force applied on it.

Let's understand the concept of unbalanced force in Inertia.

As we have discussed above about two situation. The first is about no external force applied on the rest football. And the second is gravity. So here in this case of rest football on the ground. The gravitational force has cancelled by upward Normal force. Hence the resultant force will be zero. Therefore, the football has a tendency of rest called football has inertia.

Types of Inertia

According to Newton's first law of motion. The inertia can be divided into three parts.

1. Inertia of rest.
2. Inertia of motion.
3. Inertia of direction.

Today in this post we will only discuss about inertia of rest. Not only the definition but also the top 8 examples of inertia of rest that we have seen in our daily life.

All the scientific phenomenon whether it inertia, Newton's laws, thermodynamics laws, gravitation etc can be seen in our daily life style. We have to just open our scientific mind of seen.

As similar to other phenomenon that happen in our daily life. The one most common is inertia of rest. So before we discuss the examples of inertia of rest. Let's take an overview about what is inertia of rest?

What is inertia of rest in simple words

Inertia of rest is simply defined as the tendency of any body to remains the original state of rest is called Inertia of rest.

In other words, if a body is in position of rest means it is not moving from one place to another then we can say that the body has a tendency to remains in state of rest.

Inertia of rest in terms of Newton's law

The concept of inertia of rest, inertia of motion and inertia of direction comes from Newton's first law of motion.

According to Newton's first law of motion those bodies which are in state of rest remains in rest or in motion remains in motion until or unless no external or unbalanced force applied on it.

The definition is quite similar to the definition of inertia because the concept of Newton's first law and inertia is same.

Inertia is originated from Newton's first law. You can also say that inertia is the refined concept of Newton's first law.

Deep discussion on Inertia of rest

Newton discovered three laws. Galileo was the first who talked about laws of motion and gravitation. But after the death of Galileo, it was Newton who published the three laws of motion called Newton's laws of motion. After the discovery of Newton's first law, the concept of inertia came.

Now, the question is why the concept of inertia came from Newton's first law. So the answer is hidden in the definition of Newton's first law.

As we know, Newton's first law says that any body which have a state of rest to remains in rest or which have a state of motion it also remains in motion. For example if a body is moving, it doesn't means some force is responsible for moving that body. It is the tendency of that body to keep moving forever until or unless no external or unbalanced force applied to it.

As we know the definition of inertia of rest is extracted from Newton's first law. Now, the meaning of inertia is also quite similar to the meaning of mass. That means if a body has some masses, then it has also some inertia.

So we can say that inertia is a type of force that can be experienced when the state of body changes. For example if we sit in a bus which is in rest. And if the bus suddenly start moving we will experience some backward force because of inertia of rest. Hence, we conclude that inertia is also a type of force.

Property of inertia of rest

These are some properties that describe the inertia of rest.

The first property of inertia of rest of a body is that it resist the change in their state of motion.

The second property of inertia of rest of a body is that some forces are necessary to apply to move the rest body.

The last property is that when a body is at rest. It has a definite amount of inertia due to certain mass of the body.

Factors depends on inertia of rest

There are two simple factors that the inertia of rest of a body depends.

The first factors that affect Inertia of rest is mass of a body. Means more the masses of a body. More will be inertia and less will be mass the less will be inertia.

The second factors that affect Inertia of rest is density of a body. More will be density the higher will be inertia and vice versa.

One experiment to demonstrate inertia of rest

To perform this experiment take one glass, one square playing card and one 5 rupees coin.

Now, we have all the things that is necessary to perform the experiment of inertia of rest. We will perform this experiment in five simple steps. So let's start.

Step 1 :- Take one 5 rupees coin, one square size playing card and one glass.

Enter Caption

Step 2 :- Now, placed this card on the above of the glass filled with water.

Step 3 :- After placing the card, let's place teh coin above the card.

Enter Caption

Step 4 :- Pull the playing card suddenly in backward direction.

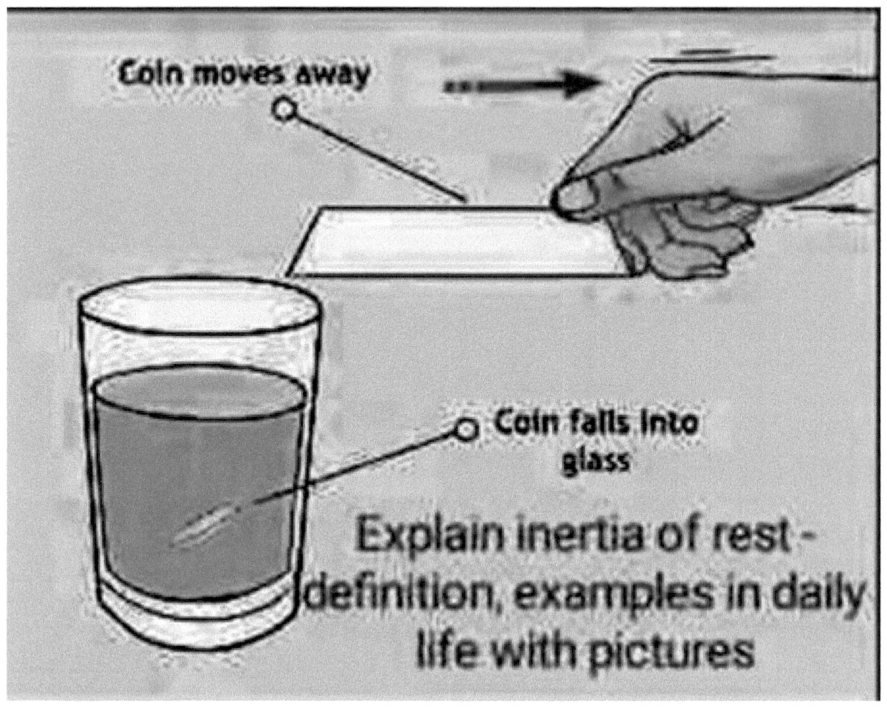

Enter Caption

Step 5 :- After pulling it in inward direction the coin falls down vertically in the glass. This is because the original state of the coin was at rest. But after suddenly pulling the card. The card Start moving in backward direction. But card has a tendency to remains its state of rest. So it falls down vertically. This shows that the coin follows the concept of inertia of rest.

8 most common examples of inertia of rest in our daily life.

Here are the 8 examples of inertia of rest with explanation that we experiences in our day to day life.

1. Felling jerk after bus start moving.

This happens as follows, when we sat on a stop bus and if the bus start moving suddenly then we feel a background jerk in our body. This is due to the inertia of rest. Because the bus get motion but our body has the tendency to remains it in state of rest.

2. Coin drop vertically when the card flick.

Now, take a playing card, a coin and a glass of water. Put the card on the top of the glass and put coin on the card. Now, flick or pull the card in the backward direction. You will find that due to the suddenly pulling of the card, the coin drop into the glass filled with water.

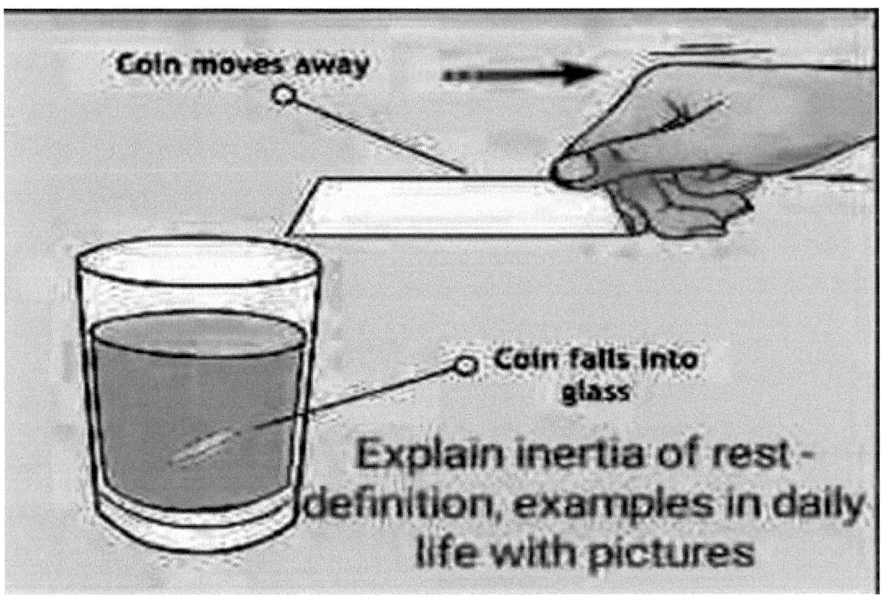

Enter Caption

This happen as follows When we put coin and card on the glass. All these things was in state of rest. But after the we have pulled the card, we applied a force only on the card not the coin placed above the card. So due to the tendency of the coin to remains in original state i.e, rest. The coin falls vertically into the glass.

3. Dust appear after shaking of dirty clothes.

You have must seen that when we beat the dirty clothes or blankets with sticks. Or even if we shake dirty clothes with our hands in sunlight. The dust particles appears to moving in surrounding of clothes. Have you ever be think, why this happens. So this happens because of inertia of rest of dust particles.

This happens as follows, when we start beating the dirty clothes. The the cloth start moving in to and fro motion but the dust particles remains in state of rest. So due to not moving of dust particles with cloth it seems like moving in surrounding.

4. Bullet makes a fine hole in glass

This example is very interesting. You have seen in many movies that when a person shoots a glass door with gun. The bullet of the gun makes a fine hole to the size of the bullet without breaking the glass.

This happens as follows : initially the glass of the window are in rest. But after the gun fired. The bullet strikes with the glass in a perticular are with respect to the size of the bullet. And dur to the very high speed of the bullet. The glass piece from that area where the bullet strikes goes with the bullet and makes a fine hole.

5. Glass not falls after table cloth removed.

Many magician performed this magic in different different show. You have must seen that magic.

Let's perform that magic. Take a glass of water. Placed it on the table with table cloth.

Now, pull the table clothes with high force. You will notice that the glass filled with water not drop. Even their water. So how this happens.

This happens as : when we suddenly pull the table clothes. The cloth get a motion and leave the tendency of rest. But the water glass was still in state of rest. Hence, due to the inertia of rest the glass not falls down after the cloth removed from the table.

6. Falling of fruits after shaking tree.

When we shake guava, or mango tree. The fruits fall down because the fruits wants to remains in state of rest.

7. Moved backward when train start from station.

When train start moving. The wheal of the train gets motion but the passenger has a tendency to remains in state of rest. Hence, it experienced a jerk in backward direction.

8. Shutter feels heavy during shop close.

If you noticed that when we pull the shutter to close the shop. The shutter feels quite heavy. This is due to the two reasons. First is due to their high mass and other is due to inertia of rest.

Before we apply a pulling force to the shop Shutter. The shutter is in state of rest. Even after applying force the shutter wants to remains at in state of rest. Hence, we feels heavy during shop close.

After a long discussion on Inertia of rest. The time has come to talk about inertia of motion. Not only the definition but also 10 examples of inertia of motion that we have all experienced in our day to day life.

But before we go further, let's make a table of contents for this post.

Topic covered in this lecture

What is an Inertia of motion?

Formula of inertia of motion.

Q. What is inertia give an example of inertia of motion also explain which of the following has more inertia an empty box or a box full of books?

Daily life examples of inertia of motion with visual picture.

Application of inertia of motion.

Where is Inertia of motion came from?

Why inertia of motion related to Newton's first law of motion?

All the above topic are well explained in the following notes. So let's start.

What is inertia of motion?

If we talk about only inertia, neither rest nor motion. Then it is a tendency of a body to keep their original state.

So, Inertia of motion is defined as the tendency of a body to keep their original state of motion forever. Untill or unless an external force is applied to it.

Please note that :- In inertia of motion, the direction of the moving object also constant. Means will be moving in only one direction forever.

Let's take an example to understand the inertia of motion more clearly.

Case 1:-

Suppose a car is running on a straight road at a speed of 40 km/h. After 5 hours of constant moving, a curve turning has come. Now, if we didn't apply the external force (or brake) the car will be accident.

But if we apply the brake to the car, suddenly we feel a forward jerk. This jerk is because of inertia of motion.

This explains as follows : When we apply the brake the car has stopped but our body has a tendency to keep their original state of motion. Due to this we feel jerk in the forward direction.

Case 2:-

Suppose the same car is running on a straight road at a speed of 40 km/h. After 3 hours of constant moving a road breaker has come.

Now, when the car cross the breaker, the wheel of the car leave the ground for some minor second and after that it again touches the ground. But due to this we felt a jump inside the car.

This jump is because of inertia of motion. This explains as follows:

While the constant moving of the car. Our body is in state of rest with respect to other person inside the car. But in motion with respect to the people who has seen from outside the car.

Please note that :- This case is also a good example of rest and motion are relative terms.

So, after crossing the road breaker our body gain some motion but after some micro second it again touches the ground. So we felt jump in upward direction.

Case 3:-

Suppose, we are sitting in the same car. After some time, if we change the direction of the car. We felt down in the right side because of the inertia of direction.

formula of inertia of motion

Please note that there is no definite formula to calculate the inertia of motion, rest or direction.

Inertia is a phenomenon in science. It is not a mathematical concepts or equations.

The inertia of momentum has a formula. But not inertia of motion.

Inertia of motion is used to understand the concept of the questions. Inertia can be used to clean the concept of Newton's first law of motion.

Q. What is inertia give an example of inertia of motion also explain which of the following has more inertia an empty box or a box full of books?

In most simple words, Inertia is the tendency or behaviour of a body that helps them to keep their original state unless or until an external force is applied to it.

Please not that the body may be in state of rest or motion.

Example of inertia of motion.

Applying brake suddenly when the car is in motion. This explains as follows:

When the car is moving in a straight line at constant speed. And if we apply the brake, it goes slow down and Stop after some time. Due to the inertia of motion. Because the moving car always wants to remains in motion as according to Newton's first law. But when we apply brake, Newton's law break. That's the reason we feel forward force after applying brake.

Now, the question is which has more inertia.

1. An empty box.

2. A box with full of books.

Hence, to answer this question. Let's first understand that the object which has more masses has more inertia than the lighter one.

So, here the box full of books has more inertia than the empty box.

Daily life examples of inertia of motion with visual picture

1. Feel backward force when car suddenly start.
2. Feel forward force when car suddenly stops.
3. Collision of moving objects in space.
4. Moving of satellite in space.
5. Moving of planets in space.
6. Jump from moving train.
7. Objects come to you when throw inside the moving train.
8. Athletes not stop running even after reach to the final position.
9. The moving of bike for some time, even we off the engine.
10. Continuous moving of stone attached with thread in circular path.

These are the 10 most common and familiar examples of Inertia of motion that we have expressed in our life.

Application of inertia of motion

- Application of car brakes, train brakes etc works on the inertia of motion.
- The runner athelete also uses the application of inertia of motion for long jumping.
- The scientist also uses the application of inertia of motion in space satellite.

- The study of the motion of earth and other planets can be understood by the application inertia of motion.
- Aeroplane take off and landing is also use application of inertia of motion.

Why inertia of motion related to Newton's first law

According to Newton's first law of motion, a rest body always remains in state of rest and a moving object always in state of motion.

Hence, inertia of motion said that, a body which is moving with some velocity. It always moving forever until or unless an external force is applied to it.

So, the definition of both the term are inter relative. Not only the definition but also the concept of both the terms are co-related.

Linear momentum

It is measured by the products of the mass of the particle and its velocity. If m is the mass of the particle and V its linear Velocity then its momentum is P = mv

Momentum is denoted by P.

It is a Vector quantity.

If the direction of momentum is same as that of Velocity.

S.I unit of momentum P = mv.

What is Linear momentum?

P = g cm/s.

S.I unit of momentum is kg m/s.

C.G.S unit of momentum is g cm/s.

Case – I

If m = constant then $p \alpha v$. It means that if two different bodies have same mass then momentum will be greater for the body moving faster.

Case-II

If V = Constant. Then $p \alpha m$.

It means that if the body have same speed the momentum will be greater for heavy bodies.

In P = mv

If M > m then PM > pm. It means that heavier one has greater momentum.

Case – III

If two objects have equal momentum i.e. P = constant then

Example :- Question :-

A body of mass 3kg is moving with a velocity of 2m /s in the east direction. What is the linear momentum of the body? What is its direction?

P = mv.

P = 3× 2

P = 6kg m/s. towards east.

Q. How much momentum will a dumb-bell of mass 10kg transfer to the floor if it falls from a height of 80 cm? Take its downward acceleration to be 10m /s2.

U = o, h = d = 80cm, Acceleration = g = 10 m/s2

V2 = u2 + 2as,

V2 = 02 + 2× 10×80100

V2 = o+20×80100

V2=16

V=16

Newton's Second law of Motion

According to Newton 2nd Law of motion the rate of change of momentum of a body is proportional to the external force acting on it and takes place in the direction of force.

According to Newton's 2nd law :-

Force α Change in rate of momentum. Or

F α Δ PΔ+

Or

F αΔ (m v)Δ+

Since the mass of the body remains Constant for small velocities and momentum is measured by the product of mass and velocity , the momentum can change only due to the change in velocity.

F α mΔ vΔ+

We know that rate of change of velocity with respect to time is known as acceleration.

Δ V Δ+ =a

Or, F α ma.

Or, F = Kma

Where K=Constant of proportionality.

If m=1, a=1, then F=1.

Put this value in equation

F = k×1×1

1 = k×1

From equation (i) and (ii)

F = ma

K = 1

Meaning of arrow :-

The direction of acceleration of a body is same as that of the force acting on it.

Q. A body of mass 2kg is pulled by a constant force so that its acceleration is 1 m/s2 towards north. Find the magnitude and direction of the force.

F= ma.

F=2N,towards north

F=2×1

Q. A hockey ball of mass 200g travelling at 10m/s is struck by a hockey stick so as to return it a long its original part with a velocity at 5m/s calculate change of momentum occurred in the motion of the hockey ball by the force applied by the hockey stick.

M= 2001000 kg, u= 10m/s.

V= -5m/s.

Change in momentum= mv-mu.

m (v-a)

=2001000×(-5-10)

=15×-15

= -3 kg m/s

Q. An object of mass 100kg is accelerated uniformly from a velocity of 5m/s to 8m/s in 6 second. Calculate the initial and final momentum of the object, also find the magnitude of the force exerted on the object.

Mass of the object = 100kg,

U = 5m/s, V = 8m/s, T = 6 sec.

Acceleration = (V-Ut)

= (8-56)

= 36

= 0.5m/s2

Force = ma

F = 100 ×0.510

F = 50N

Rate of change of momentum = mv – mu = m(v-u)

Initial momentum = mu

= 100 × 5

= 500m/s

Final momentum = mv.

= 100 × 8

= 800m/s

Q. Two objects each of mass 1.5kg are moving in the same straight line but in opposite direction. The velocity of each object is 2.5 m/s before the collision during which they stick together, what will be the velocity of the combined object after the collision.

m1u1 + m2u2 = m1v1 + m2v2

1.5×2.5+1.5×-2.5=v1.5+1.5

1.5×2.5-1.5×2.5=v 3.0

0 = 3v

V = 0m/s.

Unit of Force

The force is expressed eighter in absolute or in gravitational units.

Absolute unit of Forces:-

An absolute unit of force which produces in a unit mass for a unit acceleration.

The absolute unit of force is in CGS system and SI system are dyne and Newton. (Expressed by the symbols dyne and N).

Dyne and Newton both the words are well known to us. We all study about that in class 9. But If we have remembered that there would be a relation exist between Dyne and Newton. So before we start discussing about relation. we should have recall both the terms Dyne and Newton in detail. After that we not only established the relation between Newton and Dyne but also derive the relation.

What is Newton?

Newton is the S.I unit of force. Which is denoted by N. Apart from this concept. Newton was a scientist. He discovered gravitation, and also very famous three laws of motion. He also write some novel on optics, calculus etc.

One Newton is defined as: A body of mass 1 kg travelling with the acceleration of 1m/s2. means 1 N = 1kg ✖ 1m/s2.

F = ma

Newton = kg . m/s2.

What is Dyne?

It is the C.G.S unit of force. It is denoted by "Dyne". If we define one dyne then it is a body of one gram of mass travelling with the acceleration of one centimeter per second square. i.e, 1 Dyne = 1g ✖ 1cm/s2.

F = ma

Dyne = 1g . cm/s2

Relation between Dyne and Newton

The mathematical relation between Newton and Dyne is, one newton is equal to the ten to the power five dyne. i.e,

1 Newton = 10^5 Dyne

In other words, the main relation between newton and dyne is both the term has same property. Means both have a unit of Force. But the difference is one have S.I unit and other is C.G.S unit.

S.I unit of force is Newton

C.G.S unit of force is Dyne.

Derivation of relation between Newton and Dyne

Here below are the derivation of relation between Dyne and Newton.

As we know that Force is the product of mass and acceleration. That means in mathematical terms F = ma. we also studied that force is the cross product of mass and acceleration.

F = ma

Force = mass x acceleration

Force = kg x m/s2 --------------- (1)

Now, change it in C.G.S unit. then,

Force = 1000 gram x 100 cm/s2 ------------ (2)

From equ. 1 and 2 we get,

1 kg x 1 m/s2 = 1000 gram x 100 cm/s2

1 Newton (from the definition of one newton) = 1000 x 100 x 1 gram . 1cm/s2

1 Newton = 10^5 x 1 gram . 1 cm/s2

1 Newton = 10^5 x 1 Dyne (from the definition of 1 Dyne)

1 Newton = 10^5 Dyne

Hence, the relation between Dyne and Newton is 1 Newton = 10^5 Dyne.

Gravitational or Practical Unit of Force

A gravitational unit of force is defined as the force with which a body of unit mass is attracted by the earths towards its center.

The gravitational unit of force in CGS system and SI unit are gram Force and kilogram Force (also called gram weight) and Kilogram weight respectively.

Newton's First laws of motion is contained in the second law of motion

According to the Newton first law of motion the position of object does not change if external force is not applied.

So if no external force is acting on the body then,

F = 0 N

Now, According to 2nd law of motion

F = ma

a = Fm

a = 0m

a = 0

= v2 – v1t2 -t1 – 0

= v2 – v1 = 0

V2 = v1

It means that if no external force is applied on a moving object then its initial and final velocities are equal. i.e, there is no change in the state of motion or velocity.

Hence, we can say that first law of motion is contained in the second law of motion.

What is Impulse?

Or Change In Momentum :- The Impulse of a force acting on a body is equal to the product of the force and the time for which it acts on a body.

A Force which acts upon a body for a very short time is called an impulsive force.

Impulse as the product of force and the time for which the force acts and its is equal to the total change in momentum.

It is denoted by I.

$I = F \times t$

Impulse is a vector quantity. Its direction is same as that of change in momentum of force.

Impulse = Change in momentum

$F \times t = mv - mu$

$F \times t = m(v-u)$

Application of Impulse

While catching a fast moving cricket ball, the players lower his hands along with the ball.

A person falling from a certain height, receive more several injuries if he falls on a cemental floor while, if he falls on a heap of sand or cotton, he had no injuries.

One more examples to illistrate our confusion on impulse. Lets suppose an athelet after finishing a race, runs for a while and stops. He does not stop in its final potision where race ends. He takes some more distance, due to the momentum of his body called impulse or impulsive force.

Newton's Third law of Motion

According to Newton's third law of motion for every action there is an equal and opposite reaction.

Action and reaction do not cancel each other because they acts on different bodies.

Force always occur in pair.

$N = mg$

Action and reaction acts simultanously out of the pair of forces only force can be called action and the other reaction.

Examples of Newton's third law

During acceleration of a car the tyre pushes on road and road also pushes back the tyre.

Second example, A rocket pushes on the exhaust gas and it turn the exhaust gas pushes back to the rocket so that rocket moves.

Laws of conservation of momentum

According to the laws of conservation of momentum total initial momentum is equal to final momentum.

$m1u1 + m2u2 = m1v1 + m2v2$

Application :-

1. Recol of Gun
2. Suddenly start the car at high speed in plane ground.

-------- Team Science laws ----------

IV

Sound And its Laws

What is sound?

sound is a form of energy.

All vibrating body produced sound.

sound is that form of energy which makes us here.

Characteristic of sound

Sound needs a material medium to travels.

Medium:- The substance through which sound travels is called a medium.

Note:- Hence we can say sound can travels through a medium solid, liquid and gasses, but it cannot travels through vaccum.

Sound can travels through solid

If a child speaks into one tin he can be here by another child who puts his ear to the other tin. It means that sound can travels through solid.

Sound can travels through liquid

If we fill a balloon with water and hold it near our ear then hit by a finger in lower side of the balloon with some force then we observe that some is hearing, so we conclude by this experiment when we git balloon then water molecules vibrate up and down rapidly and we here sound.

it means that sound can travels through water.

Sound can travels through gasses

When our parents talk to each other then we here sound because of disturbance of the particles of the air. we know that air is a gas so, sound can travels through gas.

it is the same reason for telephone bell when it ring.

Sound can't travels through vaccum

A material medium (like air) is necessary for propagation of sound.

The case of moon and the outer space this happens as follows:-

In outer space there is no air present so we know that for propagation of sound a material medium must be able to carry sound waves from one place to another place but there is no material medium is present so sound cannot travels through vaccum. also sound cannot be hered in outer space or even in any place where air is not present then sound cannot travels on there. for propagation of sound there is very - very necessary a material medium like air.

We cannot be talked on the moon like on the earth so space man can talk by radio wave. radio wave can travels through vaccum or in empty space because it an electromagnetic wave. we discuss about electromagnetic waves in latter topic.

Sound travels in the form of waves

sound travels in the form of wave or even light also travels in the form of waves. we all know that sound is a form of energy so wave carry energy. wave is a vibrating disturbance in the air which carry energy from one place to another place.

Sound is a disturbance in the the medium and it is also a form of energy so sound wave carry energy from one point to another point.

If we through a stone into a pond then we saw a concentric circle in the pond produced that is called the wave of sound namely transverse wave.

when a water waves passes over the surface of the water in a pond, there is no actual movement of water from the center to the side of the pond only the water molecules vibrates up and down about their fixed positions due to this reason water molecules appears to be moving to us.

A periodic disturbance produce in a material medium due to the vibrating motion of the particles of medium is called wave.

Wave motion:-

It is the movement of disturbance produce to in one part of a medium to another involving the transfer of energy but not the transfer of matter, is called wave motion.

example:- Formation of ripples on the water surface. and propagation of sound wave through air or any other material medium.

Characteristic of wave motion

In wave motion the particles of the medium vibrate about their mean position. the particls of the medium do not move from one place to another place.

A wave motion travels by the same speed in all direction from the sound producing object in any medium.

In wave motion medium do not moves but the disturbance travels through the medium.

During a wave motion energy is transfer from one point of the medium to the another there is no transfer of matter through the medium.

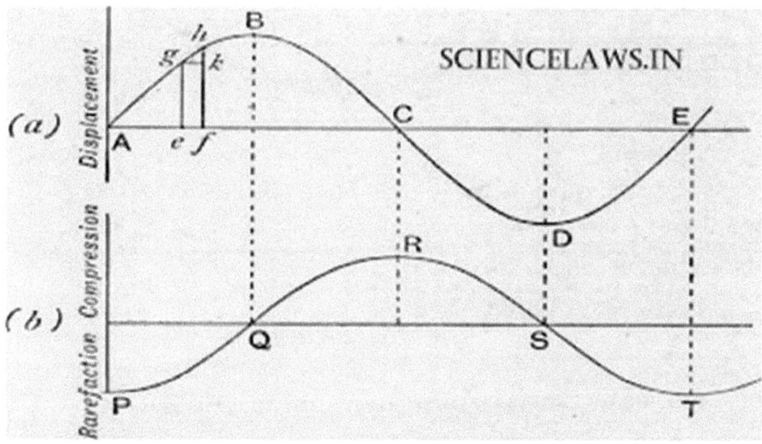

wave motion Graph

Mechanical wave and Non mechanical wave

Mechanical wave:-

- The wave which need a material medium for their propagation are called mechanical wave.
- The medium may be solid, liquid or gas.
- Mechanical wave propagate through a medium due to the elastic properties of the medium due to this reason mechanical wave are also called elastic wave.
- Mechanical waves cannot travels through vaccum.
- Mechanical waves may be longitudinal, transverse wave.
- Speed of mechanical waves are low and depends upon the source and the medium through which they travels.
- Mechanical waves are due to the vibrations of the particles of the medium.
- Example of mechanical waves are sound waves and water waves.

Non mechanical wave:-

- The wave which do not need any material medium for their propagation of the sound is called non mechanical wave.
- Non mechanical wave can also travels through a material medium as well as vaccum.
- Electromagnetic waves are also called non mechanical waves.
- Light waves are non mechanical waves.
- Non mechanical wave can travels through vaccum.

Electromagnetic wave :-

The wave which are associated with oscillating electrical and magnetic field and which do not need any material medium for the propagation of sound are called electromagnetic wave.

electromagnetic wave can even travels through vaccum. ex. light waves, redio waves, television wave and x ray are electromagnetic waves.

Electromagnetic waves are transverse wave.

Electromagnetic waves travels with a speed of 3 x 10^8 m/s.

The speed of an electromagnetic waves in any material medium is less then that in vaccum.

Sound waves travels with low speed about 344 m/s at 20° C in air.

Light wave and radio wave travels with velocity of light.

Longitudinal wave and Transverse wave

Longitudinal wave:-

In this wave particles of the medium vibrate to and fro about their mean position in the direction of propagation of the wave is called a longitudinal wave.

SCIENCELAWS.IN

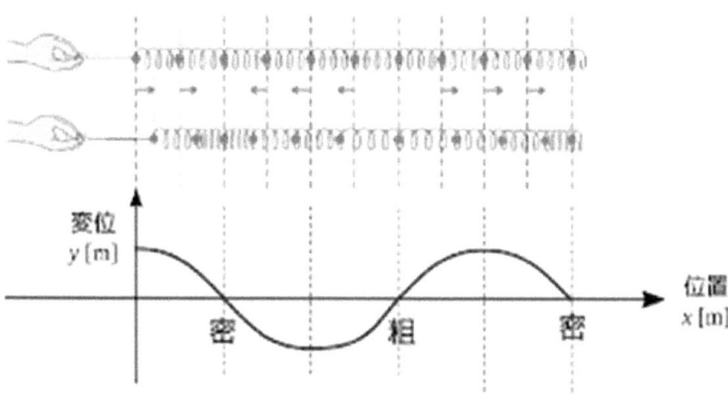

Enter Caption

The wave which travels along a spring when it is pushed and pulled at one end are called longitudinal wave.

Longitudinal wave can be produced in any medium (like solid, liquid or gas) . ex:- when a sound wave passes through air the particles of air vibrate back and forth parallel to the direction of sound wave.

When the vibrating particles come closer to one another then their is a movementry reduction in volume and a compression is formed, on the other hand when the vibrating particles apart from one another then they normally their is a movementry increases in volume and a rarefaction is formed.

Experiment to show that how compression and rarefaction is formed in air.

SCIENCELAWS.IN

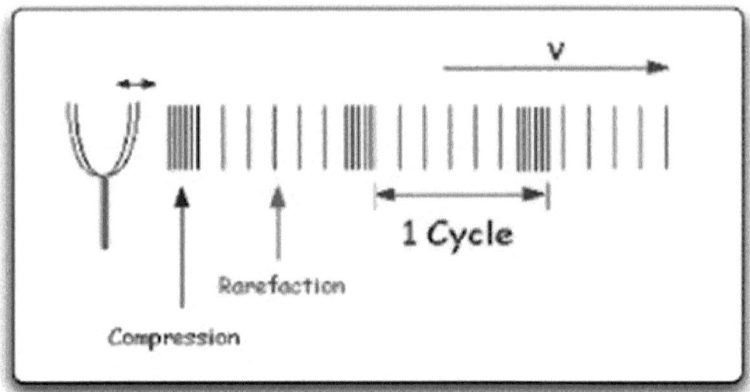

Enter Caption

Compression:-

It is the part of a longitudinal wave in which the particles of the medium are closer to one another.

Rarefaction:-

It is the part of a longitudinal wave in which the particles of the medium are further apart from the normal is called rarefaction.

Transverse wave:-

A wave in which the particles of the medium vibrate up and down at right angle to the direction in which the wave is moving is called a transverse wave.

Transverse wave can be produced only in solid and liquid but not in gas.

Example:- when a stone is droped in a pond of water, transverse water waves are produced on the surface of water. even the light wave and radio waves are transverse wave because this wave cannot travels through air we know that transverse wave also cannot consist of medium gases.

A transverse wave travels horizontally in a medium, the particles of the medium vibrate up and down in the vertical direction.

The wave propagates in the form of crest and trough.

These waves can travels through solid and on the surface of liquid only, as the propagation of these waves causes change in the shape of the medium.

As there is no vibration of volume, there is no vibration in the density of the medium while the wave propagates through it.

There is no created in pressure in the medium while the wave propagate.

Transverse wave described Graphically

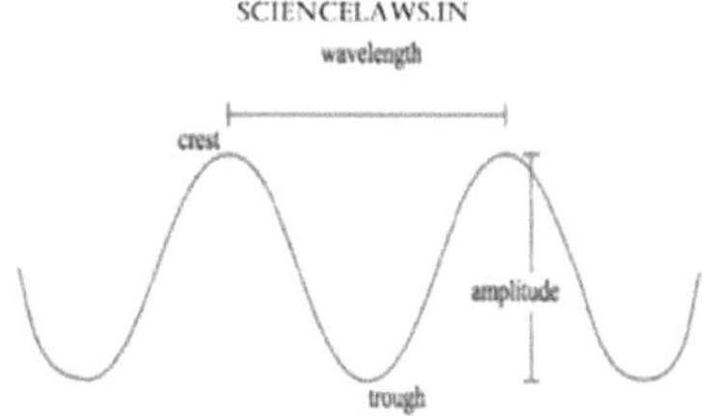

Enter Caption

Crest;-

The point of maximum position displacement on a transverse wave is called a crest.

Trough;-

The point of maximum negative depth displacement on a transverse wave is called trough.

characteristics of sound waves

characteristic of a sound wave:- A sound wave can be described by five characteristic these are

1. Wavelength
2. Amplitude
3. Time period

4. Frequency
5. Velocity

Wavelength:-

The distance between the two nearest crest of a wave is called its wavelength.

The minimum distance in which a sound wave repeats itself is called its wavelength.

In other words it is the length of one complete wave.

The distance between neighboring crest and trough is equal to half of the wavelength.

Wavelength is denoted by lambda (λ).

S.I unit of wavelength is 'm' .

Amplitude:-

The height of the crest or the depth of the trough of a wave is called amplitude.

It is denoted by 'A'.

Its S.I unit is 'm' .

The amplitude of a wave is a measure of its energy hence the greater of the amplitude of a wave the greater is the energy.

Frequency:-

The number of wave produced per second is called frequency.

Frequency is denoted by ? or read as (nu) or f.

The unit of frequency is Hz.

example:- If 30 waves cycle are produced in one second then the frequency of the periodic wave is 30 Hz or 30 cycle/s.

Note:- Frequency of a wave does not depend upon the nature of the medium through which it is travels hence the frequency of the wave remains the same as like solid, liquid and gas.

Time period:-

The time required to produce on complete wave is called the time period of the wave.

The S.I unit of time period is second 's' .

It is denoted by letter 'T'.

Wave velocity:-

The distance traveled by wave in one second is called wave velocity.

It is denoted by letter 'V'.

The S.I unit of wave velocity is m/s.

The velocity of the wave depends upon the material medium through which they travels.

speed of sound in air 343 m/s at 20 degree C.

Speed of sound depend on medium as I say in the previous line.

Relation between Time period and its frequency

We know that time required to complete one wave is called time period.

Number of wave produce in 'T' sec. = 1

Number of wave produce in 1 sec. = 1/T

but,

we know that No. of wave produce in one second is called frequency,

∴ Frequency = 1/ time period

F = 1/ T

Relation between wave velocity, Frequency and wavelength for a periodic wave.

velocity of wave = wavelength x Frequency

Sonic Boom:-

When a body moves with a velocity which is greater than the speed of sound in air then it is said to be travelling at supersonic speed. (such as jet fighter plane or bullet gun), and when they produce a sharp loud sound called a sonic boom.

Sound depends on many things.

1. Pitch
2. Loudness
3. Quality of musical sound

Pitch:-

We can distinguish between a man's voice and a women's voice of the same loudness even without seeing them. this is because a man's voice and a women's voice differ in pitch.

A man's voice is flat having a low pitch, whereas a women's voice is shrill having a high pitch.

Pitch is that characteristic of sound by which we can distinguished between different sound of the same loudness.

Pitch of the sound depends upon the frequency of the vibration.

Pitch of the sound is directly proportional to its frequency.

loudness:-

The loudness of sound is a measure of the sound energy reaching the ear per second.

Loudness of the sound depends on the amplitude of sound wave.

The greater the amplitude of sound wave , louder the sound will be.

The S.I unit of loudness of sound is decibel. ' dB '.

The softest sound which human ears can here is said to have a loudness of zero decibel.

The loudness of sound of people talking quietly is about 65 decibel.

Reflection of sound

The bouncing back of sound when it strikes on a hard surface is called reflection of sound.

Sound waves are much longer than light wave so they required a much large area for reflection.

------------------ Team Science Laws ------------------

V

Electricity

Topic covered in electricity (physics)

Types of Electric charge; SI unit of Electric charge; Coulomb; Conductors and Insulators; Electric potential and Potential difference; Measurement of potential difference; Voltmeter; Electric current; Measurement of electric current; Ammeter; How to get a continuous flow of electric current; Direction of electric current; How the current flow in a wire; Electric circuits; Relation between current and potential difference; Ohm's law; Resistance; Factor affecting resistance; Electric power; Heating effect of electric current.

What is charge?

Charge of two types:- 1. Positive charge, 2. Negative charge

- Like charge repel each other and unlike charge attract each other.
- Charge is conserved in nature.
- Charge is quantiesed in nature.
- Charge is denoted by Q.
- S.I unit of charge is Coulomb.
- Charge is scalar quantity.

Electric Potential

The electric potential at a point in an electric field is defined as the work done in moving a unit charge from infinite to that point.

It is denoted by V.

Potential difference

It is the amount of workdone to bring a unit positive charge from reference point to specific point in the electric field. without producing any acceleration.

Electric potential is denoted by V.

S.I unit of electric potential is volt.

Potential difference = workdone/ quantity of charge move

V = W / Q

If W = 1 Joule, and Q = 1 coulomb then V = 1 volt

Define 1 volt

It is defined as the when 1 joule of work is done in moving a charge of 1 coulomb from reference point to specific point is called 1 volt.

Electric current

Rate of flow of charge per unit time is called electric current.

I = Q / T

S.I unit of current is Ampere.

Ampere is denoted by A.

If charge is 1 coulomb, time is 1 second then current is 1 Ampere.

Current flowing through a conducting wire is 1 A when 1 C charge passes through conducting wire for 1 second.

Types of Current

1. Direct current or DC
2. Alternating Current or AC

Direct current or DC:-

The current whose magnitude and direction does not vary with time is called direct current or Dc.

The source of DC are Cell, Battery , and DC dianamo.

Alternating Current or AC:-

The current whose magnitude continuously change with time and periodically change its direction is called Alternating current.

Direction of Current and Electron

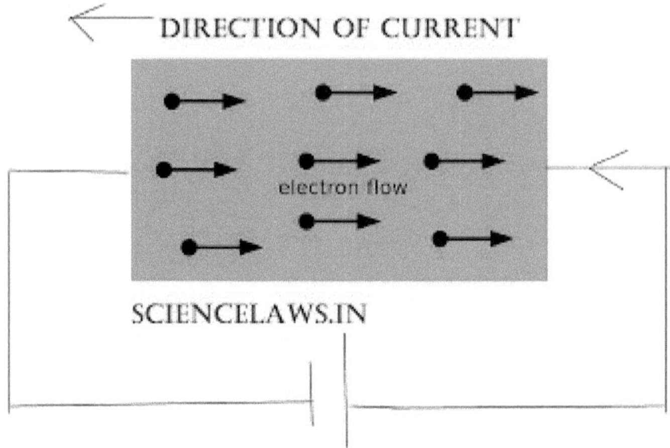

Enter Caption

Higher potential to lower potential. (direction of current)

Lower potential to higher potential (direction of electron)

Electric current:- It is the closed conducting path in which current is flow.

Voltmeter:- It is used to measure potential difference between two path.

It has high resistance.

It is connected in parallel combination.

Ammeter:-

It is used to measure electric current flowing through a conductor.

It has low resistance.

It is connected in series.

Electric circuit

A continuous conducting path consisting of wires and other resistance like electric bulb, and a switch, between the two terminal of the battery along which an electric current flow, is called a circuit.

Ohm's law

At constant temperature and pressure (physical condition remains same) the current passing through the conductor is directly proportional to the potential difference across its ends.

According to Ohm's law,

Electric current ⋉ potential difference

$I \ltimes V$

From above explanation we conclude that

potential difference between two ends ⋉ current passing through the conductor

$V \ltimes I$

$V = IR$

$R = V / I$

where R is constant called resistance

S.I unit of resistance is ohm Ω.

we find that the ratio of the potential difference and the current flowing through the conductor is a constant quantity called resistance.

the current is directly proportional to the potential difference.

the current is inversely proportional to the resistance.

If potential difference is double the electric current get double.

If resistance is double then the electric current get halved.

If potential difference is 1 V and current is 1 A then the resistance is 1 Ω.

The conductor which obey the ohm's law are called the ohmic conductor or linear resistance.

All metallic conductor such as silver, Aluminium, copper, Iron, etc. are the ohmic conductor.

All conductor which do not obey the ohm's law are called the non ohmic conductor or non linear resistance.

Limitation of ohm's law

Ohm's law does not apply to the conductor such as diode, Radio, electricity through gas etc.

Ohm's law is applicable only when the physical condition remains constant.

Factor affecting resistance

The resistance of a conductor depends on temperature, Nature of material medium, length, and the cross sectional area.

1. Temperature:- If resistance of the wire at 0 °C be R or if resistance of the wire increase then the temperature also increases.

2. Nature of material medium:- It has been found that if two resistor made up of the same length and same area of cross section but different material then the resistance is different.

3. Length:- If the length of the wire increase then the resistance also increases.

4. Area of cross section:- If area of cross section increase then the resistance decreases.

Factor affecting the Resistance of a conductor.

1. Resistivity

it has been found by experiment that,

Resistance of a conductor is directly proportional to the length of the conductor.

$R \propto L$

Resistance of a conductor is inversely proportional to the area of cross section of the conductor.

$R \propto 1/A$

$\therefore R \propto L/A$

$R = \rho L/A$

Where ρ (rho) is called the resistivity of the conductor and also known as specific resistance.

Unit of Resistivity is ohm-m (Ω-m).

Please note that resistivity of a substance does not depends on its length or thickness. It depends on the nature of the substance and temperature.

2. Combination of resistance

Resistance can be combine in two ways,

In parallel combination

In series combination

Why our house circuit is in parallel combination

If we want to increase the resistance then the combination will be in series.

If we want to decrease the resistance then the combination will be in parallel that's why in our house circuit is in parallel combination to decrease the resistance.

Resistance in series combination

The combination of multiple numbers of resistance (multiple numbers means 2,3,4,5,6,7,8 and so on...) in series combination is equal to the sum of the individual resistance.

for example if the resistances R1, R2, R3, R4,... etc., are connected in series then the resultant resistance will be,

R = R1 + R2 + R3 + R4 + R5 +.........etc.

Points to remember

When a number of resistances are connected in series then the potential difference across each resistance are different.

When a number of resistances are connected in series then the amount of electric current flowing through the each resistance are same.

Resistance in parallel combination

The reciprocal of the combined resistance of a number of resistances connected in parallel is equal to the sum of the reciprocals of the individual resistance.

for example, if the resistance R1,R2,R3,R4,R5... etc. are connected in parallel then the Resultant resistance will be,

1/R = 1/R1 + 1/R2 + 1/R3 + 1/R4 + 1/R5 + ... etc.

Points to remember

When a number of resistances are connected in parallel then the potential difference across each resistance is same which is equal to the voltage of the battery.

When a number of resistances are connected in parallel then the amount of electric current flowing through the each resistance are different.

Electric power

electric power is the electrical work done per unit time.

Power = Work done/Time taken

P = W/t

Unit of power

The power of 1 watt is a rate of working of 1 joule per second.

1 watt = 1 joule/1 second.

VI

VII

Magnetic effect of electric current

what is magnet?

It is the substance which have the property of attracting small peace of Iron, Nickle or cobalt etc. are called magnet. and this property of attraction is called Magnetism.

Magnets are found naturally in certain natural rocks and can also be made artificial by certain method.

Artificially made permanent magnet are made in various shapes like Bar magnet, Disk, Horse shoe ring.

Permanent magnet are two pole North pole and south pole.

North pole and South pole are denoted by capital letter 'N' and 'S'.

Magnetic pole:-

it is the are of the magnet where the magnetic effect are strong.

Properties of Magnet

Magnet apply force on iron filling, Nickle filling etc.

Magnet apply force on each other.

Like pole repel each other and unlike pole attract each other.

The attraction is the maximum at the end of the magnet.

Magnetic Field:-

It is the reason or area around a magnet where force of magnet can be experienced is said to be magnetic field.

Magnetic field lines:-

It is the imaginary lines, used to show the magnetic field in a given reason.

It is closed continuous curved which is directed from North pole to south pole.

Magnetic field lines never each other or do not intersect each other, because we know that direction of magnetic field towards outward is North to South but if the magnetic field intersect each other then they have two direction which is not possible at any cost.

Magnetic field has vector quantity.

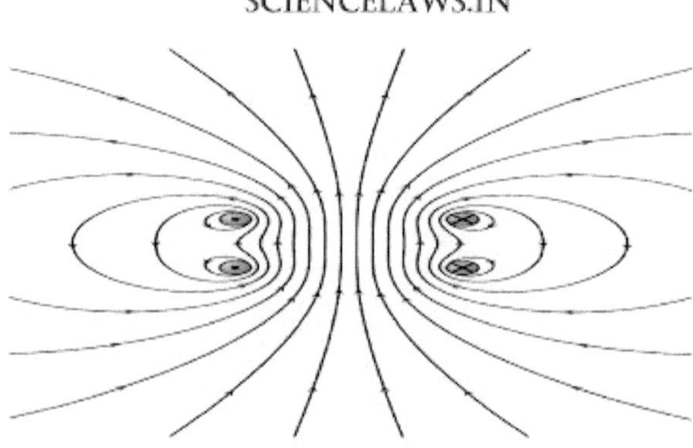

Enter Caption

Direction of Magnetic field

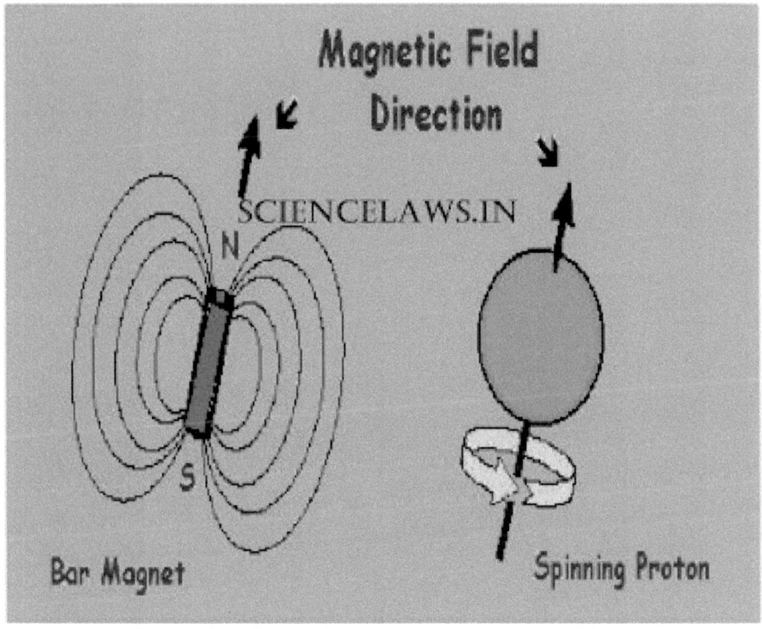

above fig. shows the concepts of direcion of magnetic field

Towards outwards
North to south
Towards inwards
South to North
maximum field lines near the pole shows the strength of magnet.
If more crowed then magnetic field more powerful at that point or vice - versa.

Magnetic field due to current carrying conductor

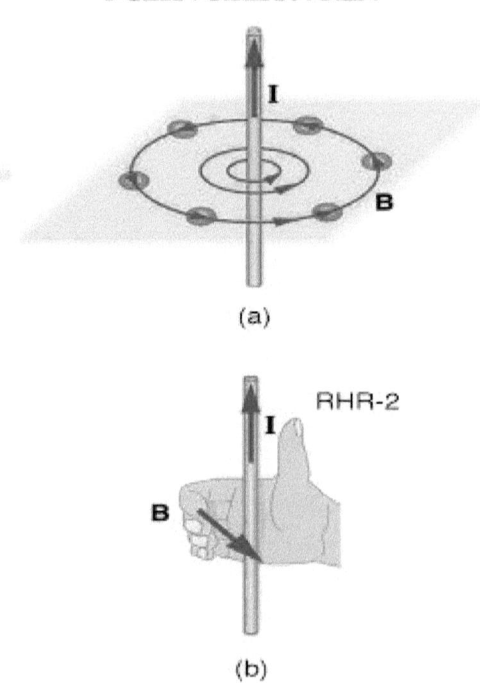

See the above fig. Magnetic field due to current carrying conductor

A current carrying straight conductor has magnetic field in the form of concentric circle around it, and it shows by magnetic field lines.

If a current in a conductor will increase, then magnetic field also increases.

$B \propto I$

If length of conductor, then magnetic field will also increases.

$B \propto L$

If distance from the conductor increases then magnetic field decreases.

$B \propto 1/R$

Now from all equations we get,

$B \propto IL/R$

Unit of Magnetic field:-

$B \propto I L / R$

When current is measure in Ampere, distance is in 'm'. then magnetic field is measure in Tesla 'T'.

or

S.I unit of magnetic field is Tesla ' T '.

Smaller unit of magnetic field is gauss 'G'.

Fleming's left hand rule:-

According to Fleming's left hand rule first finger shows the direction of magnetic magnetic field,Central figure shows the direction of electric current flowing in the conductor and the thumb shows the direction of force.

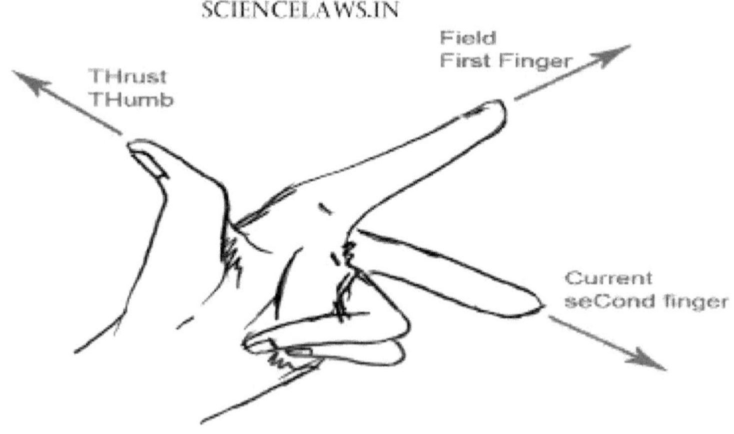

Enter Caption

Fleming's right hand rule:-

According to Fleming's right hand rule first finger soch the direction of electric field, Central finger shows the direction of induced current in the conductor and the thumbs shows the direction of motion of conductor in magnetic field.

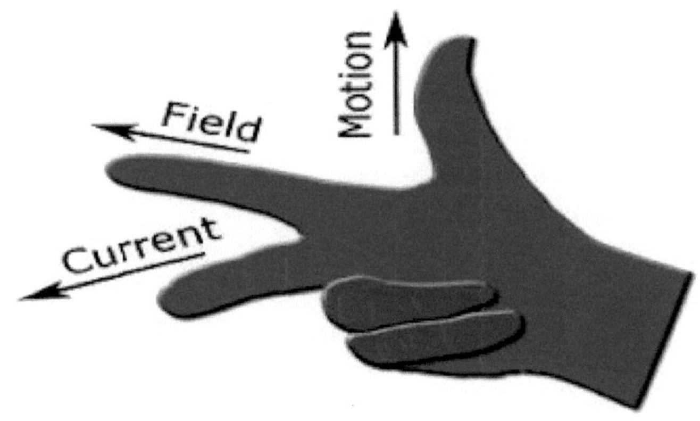

Enter Caption

what is Solenoid?

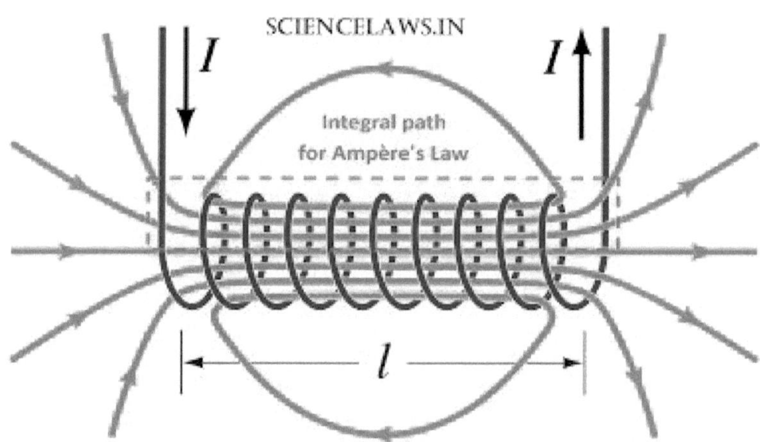

Enter Caption

It is a wire wrapped closely in the form of a helix.

It is a conducting wire of spiral shape when electricity is passed through the wire it produces magnetic field, the direction of which is directed by using the maxwell's right hand cross screw rule.

The current kich anticlockwise direction at. 'A' North pole is produced and at the end 'B' a south police produced.

Magnetic field inside the solenoid

The strength of magnetic field increase if the current flowing in the solenoid increases and vice versa.

If number of turns per unit length is increases then magnetic field also increases.

Toroid:-

A circular solenoid is called toroid.is a solenoid is banned in a circular shape and the end are joint we get a toroid.

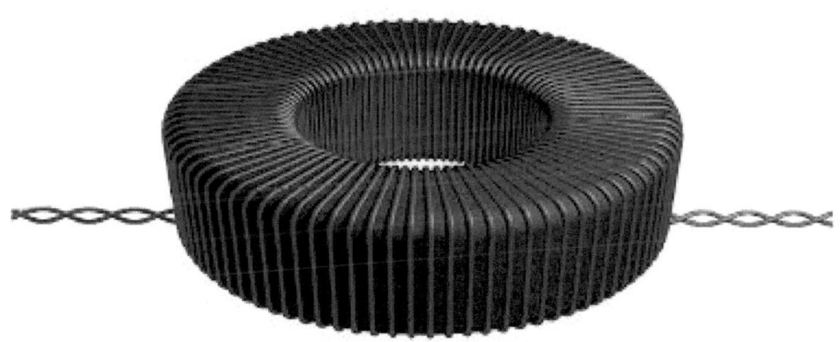

Enter Caption

Define of ampere:-

If two parallel long wires kept 1 metre apart income carry equal current in the same direction and there is a force of 2 x 10 to the power minus 7 Newton attraction of each wire the current in each wirc is sald to be one ampere.

Electromagnetic induction:-

it is the phenomenon of producing induced current in a closed circuit or coil due to the change in position of magnetic field in the nearby circuit or a closed coil.

Factor on which induced current depends:-

Induced current is directly proportional to number of turns of the coil it means that if a coil has a large number of turns then large induced current is produced in the closed coil.

Induced current is directly proportional to strength of magnet.

induced current directly proportional to speed of the coil it means that if the magnet moves very quickly than large induced current is produced in the closed coil.

Domestic electric circuit:-

The electric power is supplied to the house of factories through underground cable for overhead wire on poles.

Overhead aur Keval known as phase wire, live wire, neutral wire and Earth wire.

Difference between the live wire and neutral wire each 220 volt.

Live wire is covered with insulation of red and brown colour.

Neutral wire with an insulation of black and blue colour and the earth wire is covered with insulation of green or yellow colour.

Electric fuse:-

It is a Safety device used to save the electrical appliances like electric bulb, electrical tube TV etc. From burning when large amount of current flow in a circuit.

It is a wire made of copper-aluminium tin-lead alloy.

It has low melting point.

it is connected in series with an electrical device like bulb, TV, refrigerator, washing machine etc.

the capacity of a phase wire is a large if it is thick and capacity of the fuse wire is small if it is thin.

short circuiting takes place when the live wire and neutral wire come in direct contact.

overloading means law of large amount of current in the circuit beyond the pammicable value of current.

Aur another word when many electrical appliances of high power rating are connected in a single circuit then overloading occur.

VIII

Source Of Energy

Source of energy

It has the capacity to provide useful energy example all is an important source of energy.

Types of source of energy

Renewable source of energy:- a source of energy which can be renew again and again in the short period of time is called renewable source of energy. Example solar energy, wind energy, tidal energy etc.

Non renewable source of energy:- a source of energy which cannot be e Renu again and again in a short period of time but it can be renew over a very long period of time is called non renewable source of energy. Example Fossil fuels and nuclear fuels.

Fossils fuels:-

Those fuel which take long time for their preparation in the deep of the earth crust through the action of pressure heat and bacteria in the absence of air from the decomposition of dead plants and animals is called fossil fuel.

Fossil fuels are coal, petroleum and natural gas.

It is non renewable source of energy.

It is also known as conventional source of energy.

Coal:-

It is a mixture of compounds of carbon hydrogen and oxygen what is small amount of nitrogen and sulphur is also present in it.

Note:- India has largest deposit of coal in the Bihar Odisha Madhya Pradesh etc.

Types of coal:-

Coal are four types:-

Peat

Lignite

Betomenous

Anthracite

Uses of coal:-

It is used as a domestic and industrial fuel.

It is used in thermal power plant for generating electricity.

Note coke has 98% carbon and it is used as reducing agent in metallurgical process extraction of metal.

It is used to prepare synthetic oil and synthetic natural gas.

Petroleum:-

It is a black viscous liquid which consists mainly of hydrocarbons along with other elements such as oxygen, Sulphur and nitrogen.

It also consists of salt and rock material.

Refining of petroleum or crude oil.

It is the process of separating various component of petroleum from one another by fractional distillation or heating in the presence of air.

Fractional distillation of petroleum gives petroleum gas or LPG petrol, kerosene oil,paraffin wax diesel etc.

LPG or liquefied petroleum gas

It is petroleum gas in liquid state.

It is mixture of ethane, propane and butane but the major component is butane.

Advantage of LPG

It has high calorific value.

It does not produce smoke.

It's handling is easier as compared to coal and kerosene.

It does not produce any poisonous gas.

It is very neat and clean domestic fuel.

Precaution in using LPG

Rubber tube should be checked at regular for crack or holes.

Gas burner should be standard.

the value of the regulator of the gas cylinder should be kept closed when not in use.

Ethyl mercaptan Sulphur dioxide gas trapped easily and it is mixed with petroleum gas or LPG in small amount for preventing leakage of gas.

Natural gas:-

It is a mixture of gaseous hydrocarbon consisting of methane 85% and mixture of methane, butane, propane with traces of carbon dioxide, nitrogen, Oxygen and hydrogen sulphide.

it is found deep in the earth crust either along or along with crude oil deposit.

Advantage of natural gas:-

It is a clean fuel.

It is transported through the pipeline in the form of CNG.

It has high calorific value.

CNG compressed natural gas:-

when natural gas is compressed by applying a high pressure it becomes a liquid called compressed natural gas or CNG.

Calorific value of fuel:-

It is the amount of heat produced by burning 1 gram of fuel completely.

Ideal fuel:-

It should have high calorific value.

It should be burnt without releasing any harmful gas.

It should not leave ash.

It should be cheap, save to transport and easy to handle and use.

Note:- hydrogen is a cleaner fuel than CNG because the product of combustion of hydrogen is H2O but the product of combustion of CNG is CO2 and H2O. CO2 produce greenhouse effect.

Biogas:-

It is formed by anaerobic degradation of biogas.

The major constituent of biogas is methane 75%.

The other major gas is CO2 which traces of other gases like hydrogen sulphide H2S.

Use of biogas:-

It is used as a fuel for cooking.

It is used to generate electricity.

It helps in producing manure.

Advantage of biogas:-

It has longest life.

It has a low cost.

It has require less maintenance.

It is a renewable source of energy.

Non conventional source of energy:-

The source of energy obtained from sun is called solar energy.

Uses of solar energy:-

It is used for drying food grains ,fish, firewood etc.

Obtaining Salt from seawater by evaporation.

Solar energy device:-

It is a device which capable using solar energy directly as heat or converting it into electricity.

Device which uses of solar energy directly into electricity called solar cell.

Device which uses solar energy as heat is called solar cooker.

IX

Reflection of light

Introduction

Reflection of light is the phenomenon of natural that plays with the behaviour of light. In the further of the post we will discuss about reflection and some common examples of reflection of light in more depth ways. But before we procced we have to first know a little about reflection and how it happens in any surface weather it is rough, smooth, and curve. So let's start with what is reflection.

What is reflection of light?

Reflection is the natural phenomenon of light that seperate the light waves to go through a straight line. Means it is due to the reflection that a beam of light changes its path.

In other words the bouncing back of light wave in the same medium when strikes with any surfaces weather it is plane, curve or rough.

For example, you can see in the above fig. That a tree get reflection in water. It is happens as follows: when the rays of light falls on the tree then tree becomes luminous object and a luminous object easily get reflected in a smooth surface. Here the smooth surface is water. That's why a virtual image of tree formed in the water.

Luminous object is that object which has its own light. Means the object should be glowing or have some light in itself.

To understand the reflection of light in more detail lets see the another definition.

When a source or an object emitting the rays of light and if these rays of light get touched with any regular or irregular surface then the rays of light get bounced back and spread in all directions. Some of rays get back on its initial path, some are get diffused, some are followed the laws of reflection.

In the above definition of reflection of light. We have used many terms like regular, irregular, diffusion, and laws of reflection. So what was that terms means. because examples of reflection will not be understand if the concept of these terms will not clear. So before we start examples of reflection let's understand all the above terms one by one.

Types of reflection of light

There are many types of reflection of light in daily life. But we discuss only most common and relevant types that is,

Regular reflection of light

Irregular or diffusion of light

Multiple reflection of light.

1. Regular reflection of light

If the rays of light fall on a smooth surface and light waves get reflected in only one direction then it will be the regular reflection of light.

Regular reflection of light can also be defined as the light waves falls on a polished surface and get reflected in such a way that all the light waves will be parallel to each other.

2. Irregular or diffuse reflection of light

If a ray of light falls on a rough surface then after reflection light waves get diffuse in all directions.

Irregular reflection of light can also be defined as when teh rays of light fall on a surface that is not polished then after reflection it will bounce back in the same medium but not each rays will be parallel to each other.

3. Multiple reflection of light

When a rays of light fall on a surface weather it is rough or polished and the surface are placed with many other polished or rough surfaces in such a way that after reflection of light from one surface the reflected rays fall on the other surface and again reflected rays of second surface falls on the third surface and so on. Then these types of reflection is called multiple reflection of light.

In short way multiple reflection of light can be defined as when a ray of light falls on surface1 and after reflection the reflected ray of surface1 falls on a surface 2 and so on. Then these types of reflection called multiple reflection of light.

See the below fig. to understand the multiple reflection of light.

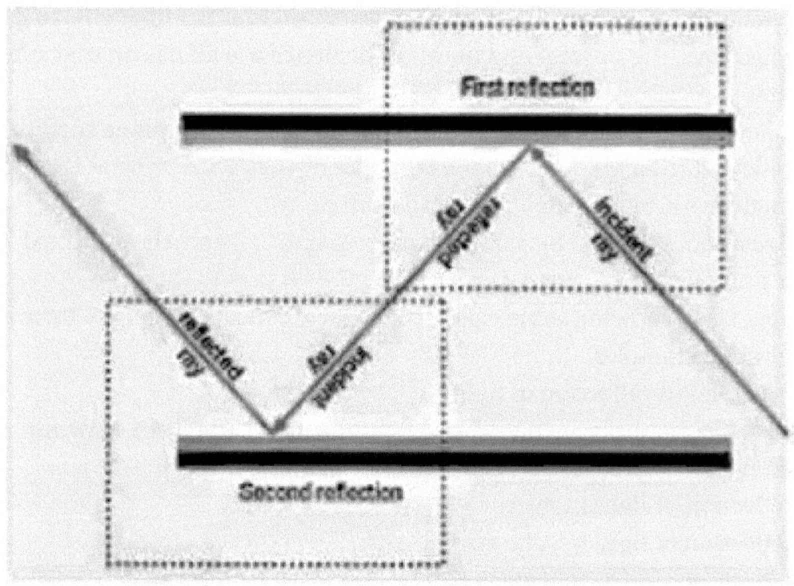

Enter Caption

In the above fig. We can see there are two surfaces named first reflection and second reflection. When a ray of light incident on the first surface it get reflected and falls on the second surface. Now the reflected ray which is falls on the second surface becomes a incident ray of second surface. So that after reflection from second surface it will again become reflected ray.

You can see the examples of multiple reflection of light in your daily life. Like if you placed a two mirror in such a way that if we bring an object between them then the image will formed in both the mirror. The best example is the mirror placed in hair cut store 'salon'.

Laws of reflection of light

We have understood the phenomena of refraction of light. Now we will try to understand how reflection occurs. Why we said that light get reflected? So to answer all of these questions. We have to first know the laws of reflection of light.

There are two laws of reflection of light.

The incidents rays, the reflected rays, the normal and the point of incidence are always lies on the same plane.

The angle of incidence is always equal to the angle of reflection.

1. First laws states that if some rays of light falls in a smooth surface and get reflected in the same medium. First laws said that the incidents rays, the reflected rays, the normal and point of incidence are all lies on that smooth surface.

2. Second laws state that when incident rays falls on a plane surface and get reflected then the angle made by incident rays with normal is equal to the angle made by reflected rays with normal.

Please note that:- The incident rays makes ∠i and the reflected rays makes ∠r. So that ∠i = ∠r.

Now, after knowing some useful concepts of reflection of light. Its time to go through examples.

Examples of reflection of light

9 most commonly seen examples of reflection of light in daily life with naked eyes.

Reflection of light in mirror.

Reflection of light in spherical mirror.

Reflection of light in water pool.

Reflection of light on polished surface.

Object seen due to reflection of light.

Glowing of stars.

Lighting of moon at night.

Reflection from luminous object.

Reflection from non-luminous objects.

Let's discuss all of the above examples of reflection of light which we can observe in our day to day life.

1. Reflection of light in mirror.

Reflection of light in mirror is the best example of reflection of light. In plane polished surface of the mirror glass the light wave reflect so well that it follows both the laws of reflection of light.

In plane mirror, regular reflection takes place. Because the particles present on the surface of the plane mirror are faced in only one direction. That's why a plane mirror shows a regular reflection of light.

But if you talk about the rough surface. The particles on the surface of the rough part are faced in many directions. That's why irregular reflection of light takes place in rough surface.

If you see the surface of the plane mirror through a microscope then you will find that the particles are faced in only one direction.

Now, let's know how a plane mirror reflects all the rays in only one directions.

So the answer is, when a beam of light falls on a smooth surface like the surface of the plane mirror. Then due to the particles faced in one particular directions, all the light waves get reflected on that direction.

See the given below fig. to learn how a plane mirror shows regular reflection of light.

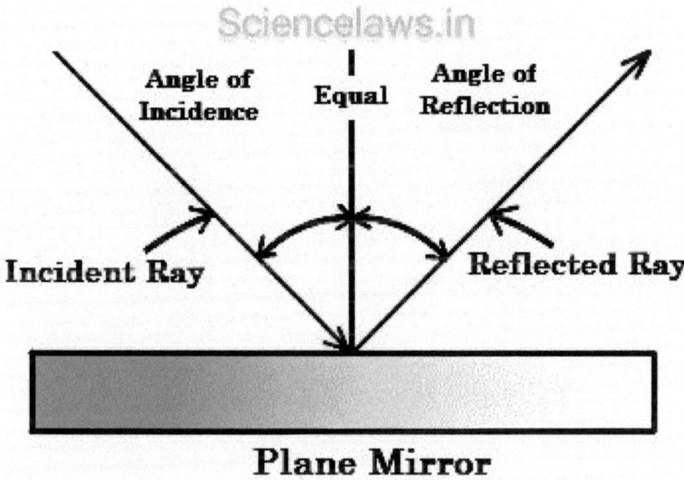

Enter Caption

In the above fig. An incident rays falls on the surface of a plane mirror and reflect. Reflection takes place in such a way that, incident rays and reflected rays makes angle of incidence and angle of reflection respectively.

Both angle of incidence and angle of reflection are equal. Because it follows the laws of reflection of light. See fig.

2. Reflection of light in spherical mirror.

After the discussion of reflection of light in plane mirror. Its time to take some knowledge about reflection in spherical mirror.

If we talk about spherical mirror. Then it is a part of a complete sphere. In simple words take a spherical ball and cut it into two pieces equally. The each cut part is like a spherical mirror.

Inner part of the cutted spherical ball is called concave. And outer surface of the cutted spherical ball called convex.

Here we will learn both, reflection in concave and reflection in convex.

Reflection of light in spherical mirror is same as in plane mirror. But it is not that simple. To understand the reflection in spherical mirror. We have to learn reflection in concave and convex mirror.

Reflection in concave mirror

As we discussed just now that reflection of light in concave mirror is same as reflection of light in plane mirror.

In a concave mirror, reflection can takes place in any part of the mirror. But it should be from inside. Because concave mirror is polished from outside. See the given fig.

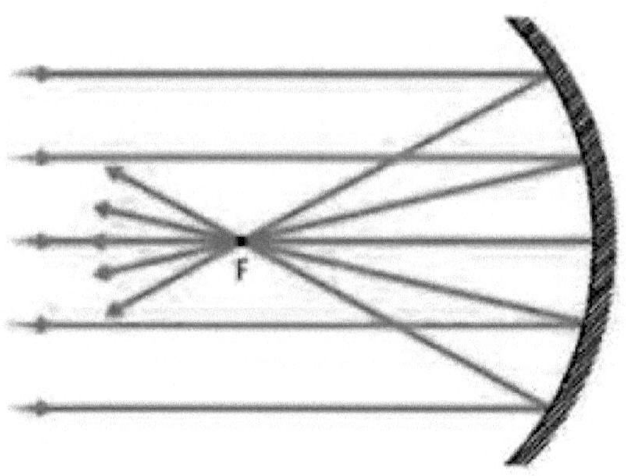

Enter Caption

In concave mirror a regular reflection of light takes place only when if it follows certain conditions. These are some conditions which must have to follow for regular reflection in concave mirror.

If the light waves are parallel to the principal axis then it the reflected rays will pass through the focus point (F).

If light waves passes through the focus then the reflected rays become parallel to the principal axis.

If the incident rays are align with the principal axis then reflected rays will returns to the same path.

As you can see in the above fig. that there are two light waves on upper side of the principal axis and two in the downward direction. All of them strikes with the inner part of the concave mirror. And after the reflection all the waves passed through the focus point. because it follows the laws of reflection of light.

Reflection in convex mirror

In convex mirror, the light waves are are also get reflected and follows the laws of reflection of light. But the reflection takes places from the outside of the mirror. Because in convex mirror, inner side is polished and outer side is shiny. That's why reflection takes place from outside.

In a convex mirror, reflection can takes place in any part of the mirror. But it should be from outside. Because convex mirror is polished from outside. See the given fig.

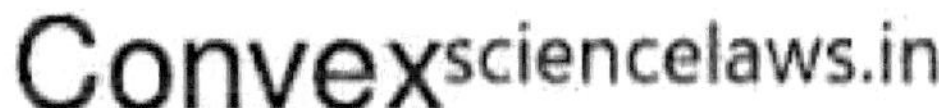

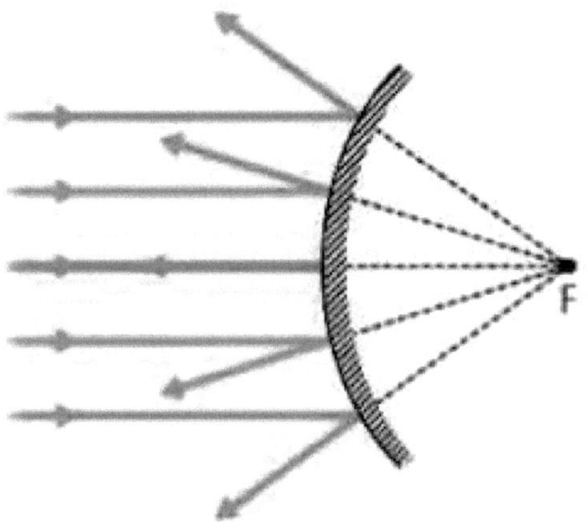

Enter Caption

In convex mirror also a regular reflection of light takes place only when if it follows certain conditions. These are some conditions which must have to follow for regular reflection in convex mirror.

If the light waves are parallel to the principal axis then it the reflected rays will pass through the focus point (F).

If light waves passes through the focus then the reflected rays become parallel to the principal axis.

If the incident rays are align with the principal axis then reflected rays will returns to the same path.

As you can see in the above fig. that there are two light waves on upper side of the principal axis and two in the downward direction. All of them strikes with the inner part of the convex mirror. And after the reflection all the waves passed through the focus point. because it follows the laws of reflection of light.

3. Reflection of light in water pool.

Reflection can also takes place in water. If you observed that, if anyone see into the water. Then an image of that object or person get virtual into the surface of the water. How this happens?

As we know reflection can takes place on both the surface. Weather it is regular or irregular. A water surface is quite regular so that when the rays of light falls on the surface of the water then some of the rays follows laws of reflection and some are not.

4. Reflection of light on polished surface.

As we know that reflection on the surface of the mirror is the best example of reflection of light. Because a mirror surface is also polished.

So on any highly polished surface, reflection can easily takes place. The best example of reflection of light on polished surface will be , reflection in stainless steel.

In vessels or stainless steel, reflection takes place. Because stainless steel has also a polished surface.

5. Object seen due to reflection.

Do you know, why we can see the objects in our surroundings? Why you are able to read this article.

The answers are due to reflection of light. But how? Let's understand.

When an object placed in the light room or to any other sources of light then it emit some source of light from itself and when these emitted light waves enters in our eyes. So that we are able to see the objects.

To seeing an object there one important thing is light. Without light it is not possible to see an object through our neked eyes.

How reflection is responsible for seeing an object?

Let suppose an object is placed in the dark room. Where there is no any sources of light.

Now placed a light bulb ? in the room. Now you can see the object very easily. But how this happens? This happens due to the reflection of light through object. Explain.

When you being a light source closer to the object. And we know that a glowing bulb emit a tons of light rays.

And when these light wave get reflected from the objects placed on that room and when that reflected rays enters in our eyes, it forms a virtual and inverted image in the retina.

After that mind correct that image and recognise. That's why we are able to see the objects in our surroundings.

6. Glowing of stars.

At night, sky are full of stars. Some of the star ??? glow brightly and some are not. But have you ever think why these stars are always seen glowing?

Starts glow because it is luminous object. But is that's it. Is this answer ok? No my dear friends. No way.

Starts are glowing because of their own light emitting from itself. But how we able to see it?

The answer is just because of the reflection of light emitted from stars. Learn how?

The glowing stars are always emitting light waves. And when these light waves travel through space and come near the earth's surface. Then it strikes with the atmosphere of the earth and at that time some of the light waves get returns into the space. But some are reflected towards the centre of the earth.

That's the reason we can see the glowing stars even it is far from us.

7. Lighting of moon at night.

Lighting of moon is also an example of reflection of light. Moon is lighting not because of it has own light. It is glowing because it reflects the light waves coming from the sun.

As we know moon is non-luminous objects. Perhaps it is glowing due to reflection of light.

Reflection takes place on the surface of the moon. And due to the irregular surface, when Sun light touches it's ground, the light waves get diffuse and some of the light enters on the earth through atmosphere.

8. Reflection from luminous objects.

Luminous object emit light waves from itself. And when these light waves collide with any other objects or non-luminous objects. Then it makes us to see that non-luminous objects.

So due to the reflection or we can say, with the help of reflection phenomenon a non-luminous objects can be seen.

In other words, due to reflection of light a non-luminous objects becomes luminous object and can emit light waves.

9. Reflection from non-luminous objects.

As we just discussed above that a reflection of light makes a non-luminous objects into a luminous object.

So it is also clear that non-luminous objects emit light due to reflection and make things visible.

Application of reflection of light.

These are the some applications of reflection of light.

Microscope works on the application of reflection of light. Because in microscope there are some small mirror piece used to see the objects.

Kaleidoscope also works on the principal of reflection of light.

The best application of reflection of light is the working of telescope. In inside of the telescope reflection takes place.

In cars side mirror.

X

Refraction of light

ntroduction on Refraction of light

In this science World. There are many natural phenomena occurs daily. One of the beautiful natural science phenomena is the formation of rainbow. During the rainy season, once in a while we must see the rainbow in the sky. But did you know how rainbow is formed? So we tell you that rainbow is formed due to the diffraction of white light through the atmosphere or cloud.

Now, we all know that rainbow is formed due to refraction. But what is meant by refraction? What did this term mean?

Refraction is the phenomena of the nature where light wave bends when travels from one medium to another medium having some difference in refractive index.

Note:- Refractive index is nothing but a measuring value that determines the amount of angle a light wave bends during the passes from one medium to another medium.

To understand the refractive index in better way. You must have to know the application of refractive index. these are :-

first application of refractive index is, it is used to measure the value of medium.

It is used to measure the wavelength of the medium.

refractive index is used in film makin process of camera.

Mobile phone display also works on the application and principal of refractive index.

In simple word refractive index is the amount that tells us how much the medium is rarer or how much is denser. For example glass is denser that air,

Diamond is denser that glass etc.

Refraction occurs in a light wave only when there is two medium available having some difference in refractive index.

Now the question is why light wave bend during travelling from one medium to another medium. Because as we studied that light travels in a straight line. Than why it bends? So the answer is very simple, when light wave travels in only one medium then it goes in a straight line. But when it passes through two different medium, it gets bend because the velocity of the light wave get increases or decreases when passes through two different medium.

Laws of refraction of light:-

First law:- According to this law, the incident ray, the refracted ray, normal and the point of incidence lies on the same plane.

REFRACTION

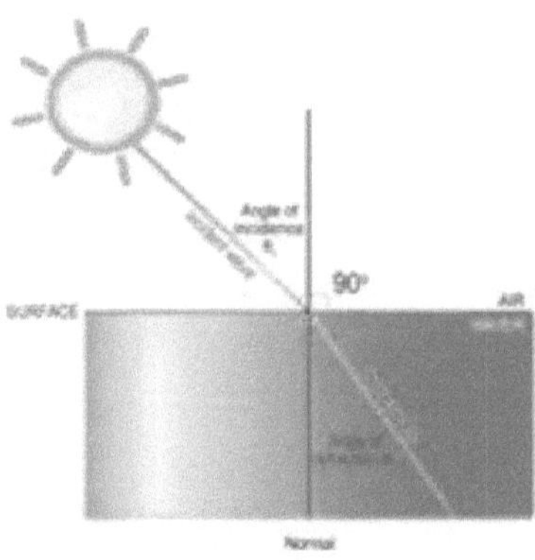

Enter Caption

Second law:- According to this law, the sine angle of incidence to the sine angle of refraction is constant. Note that this law is also known as snell's law.

Now, we knew some concept of refraction. But before we proceed in examples of refraction of light. We should have to know about the types of refraction of light.

So, generally there are total two types of refraction shown when light passes though one medium to another medium. First is in concave lens and second is convex lens.

In concave lens:-

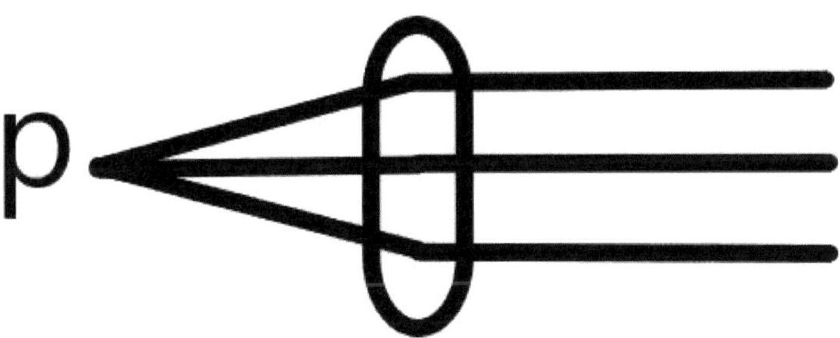

Enter Caption

In convex lens:-

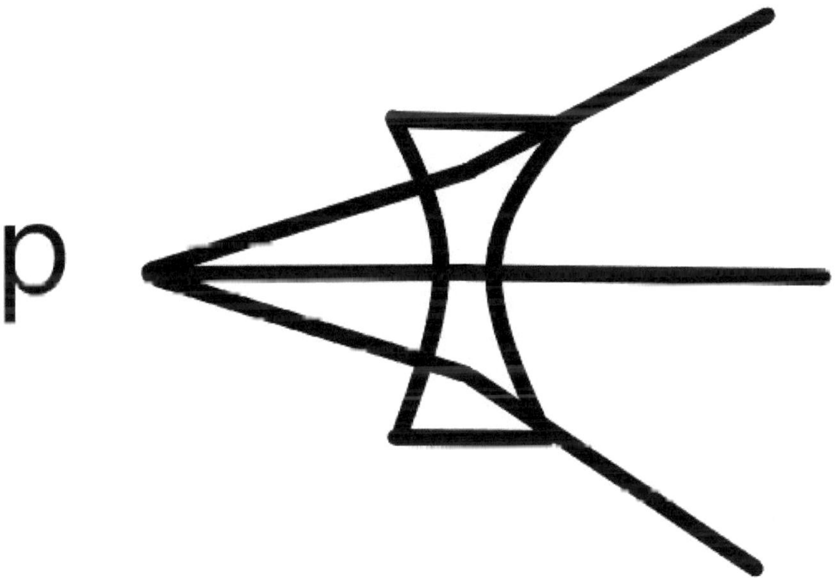

Enter Caption

So in this post we will try to understand the refraction of light in different-different way. we will also take some common examples of refraction of light that we easily observe in our day to day life. Basically these are the simple examples of refraction of light.

All these following examples are very common and must be seen at least once in your life. But you ignored it.

10 easily observable examples of refraction of light in everyday life

(1.) Refraction of light in spherical lenses.

(2.) Refraction of light in dvd.

(3.) Refraction of light in atmosphere.

(4.) Refraction of light in solid ice.

(5.) Refraction of light in water droplets.

(6.) Refraction of light in river during sunset.

(7.) Refraction in glass filled with water.

(8.) Refraction in diamond cut glass.

(9.) Rainbow is formed due to refraction.

(10.) Refraction of light in our eye lens.

Lets understand all the above examples of refraction of light that we see in our day to day life (or everyday life) one by one in detail.

(1.) Refraction of light in spherical lenses

This is one of the most famous example of refraction of light. So lets understand this example. As we know that, when light waves passes through one medium to another medium, it gets bend weather it is from rarer medium to denser medium or denser medium to rarer one. Now, we look this phenomena in spherical lenses for doing this experiment. we take both two lenses in use. First is concave lens and other is convex lens.

Case 1:- Concave Lens

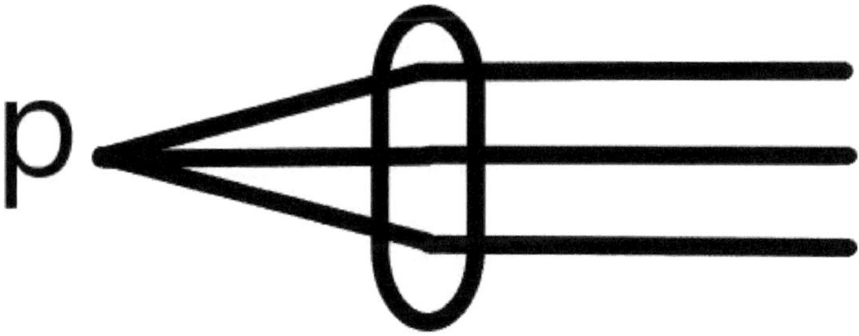

Enter Caption

In above fig. of concave lens. we can see that there are many light waves emitted from an object get bends after refraction. And all the light waves after refraction get dispersed in straight line along one direction.

In this case we use two medium first is air and second is lens which is made up of glass. So as we discussed earlier for taking place of refraction we must have difference of refractive index in medium. Hence, here is also the difference in refractive index in both medium.

Case 2:- Convex lens

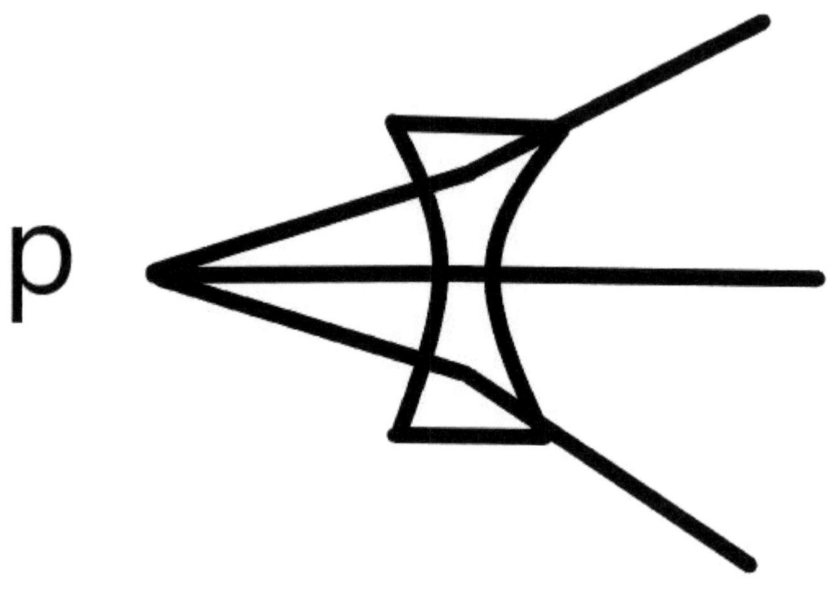

Enter Caption

In the above fig. of convex lens. we can see that there are many light waves emitted from a point 'p'. And after passing through the convex lens all these rays of light get deflected in different-different direction.

Here, in this experiment we use two medium. One is rarer which is air and other is denser which is lens. And as we studied, a ray of light when passes through two different medium get bends. So here is also same situations. All the light waves after refraction get bends.

(2.) Refraction of light in dvd

Refraction in dvd cassette is also an example of refraction of light that we can easily observe in our day to day life. Before we start please note that here we talk about transparent dvd. Not as shown in fig. Because in this type of dvd. Refraction is not possible. So take transparent dvd. Having both side clear. and looks like be glass. Don't be confuse. Your doubt will be clear after reading all short given six following paragraph.

We all uses dvd for playing music, video etc in our everyday life. But Now, the uses of dvd decreases due to increasing in technology. But we didn't forget our childhood of those days that we played with dvd. And many of the people noticed that if we see the shiny surface of the dvd in brightness of the sun. We noticed the formation of many color. So what is that color? Why we see it in brightness? Hence, the answer is very simple. The reason behind that Formation of various color is due to the refraction of height.

This happens as:- When we take dvd in closer of the brightness. The rays of light emitted from bright object enter in dvd (made up of plastics). and diverse in all direction. And due to this diversion of light various color seen.

In other words, light get refract in dvd because dvd is made up of plastics and light is coming from another source of medium (air). And we know that when light enters from one medium to another medium it get bends.

Generally, Normal dvd shows diffraction of light, because normal dvd has one side polished and other side covered with poster (or point). But what happens if we take a transparent dvd and pass a beam of light from their edge.

In that case diffraction doesn't occur. In transparent dvd light wave get passes through one side to another side. Also There will be no any formation of rainbow color. In this case we can say that refraction of light occurs in dvd. So, refraction is also occurs in dvd.

Please note that after passing beam of light from the edge of the dvd some rainbow color may be seen because of the presence of shiny crystal in dvd. So in refraction there is also may form rainbow color.

(3.) Refraction of light in atmosphere

Enter Caption

In rainy season we notice the sky looks a little like this. As shown in above fig. This phenomena of nature is due to the diffraction of light in atmosphere. But In some case when it is due to the refraction of light. This explains as follows:

After rain or during raining the sky is full of black and some white cloud. And when sun's rays falls on that cloud, some of the light rays reflect in other direction, some are disperse in all direction but some of the light rays get passes through the white transparent cloud. And this causes the refraction of light. Because when some light rays passes through the cloud. It gets bends because of traveling from one medium to another medium. Hence, refraction occurs in atmosphere.

Some people has confusion about this examples. Please note that not in case of atmosphere but also in every situation weather it is reflection, or diffraction. In every situation light wave do all three phenomena reflection, diffraction and refraction. For example whenever a light beam falls on a transparent surface. A refraction, reflection even a diffraction together happens. But at that moment we only considered those terms which we need. like here we only need the concept of refraction. So we only talk about refraction. Not diffraction or reflection. But remember, In atmosphere all refraction, reflection and diffraction occurs together.

Know How? When light falls on a surface some of the light get reflect, some are passed through the material and some are diffuse in all direction.

(4.) Refraction of light in solid ice

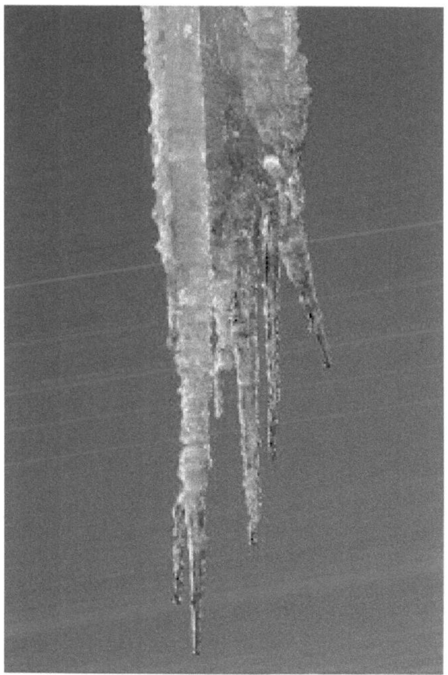

Enter Caption

Everyone has used refrigerator. Even everyone has refrigerator in their home. So you must have seen solid ice. Solid ice is made up of water. If we try to see through ice. We didn't get image properly. We will also noticed that the image is not seen clear. So why this happens? Why we cannot see image properly through solid ice? So In simple word, this is due to the refraction of light passing through solid ice.

This happens as: When a light beam travelling in a medium get enters in solid ice (which is another medium). It gets deflected from their normal lines. This is due to the decreasing in velocity of the light waves. And this causes diffraction of light.

Lets take an example to understand the concept of refraction in solid ice.

Suppose we have a polished solid ice (like a glass). And if a beam of light passes through it. It gets bends. And due to the bending of light solid ice shows refraction of light.

(5.) Refraction of light in water droplets

Enter Caption

Water droplets are spherical in shape. Also there are many water molecules present in a water droplets. As we know water droplets are spherical in shape. as shown in above fig. Due to spherical shape. It behaves like a spherical lens. And we even also know that spherical lenses are two types. First is concave and other is convex. Here we only use the term spherical instead of concave or convex.

Due to the spherical shape. When light falls on it it get refracted. Apart from refraction. Some of the light wave get diffract and some are reflect. But here we only talk about refraction. So in water droplets, refraction of light takes place.

This happens as: When a beam of light falls on spherical water droplets. light get passed through it. And during the passes of light, the velocity of the light beam decreases due to change in refractive index of the medium. Hence, refraction of light takes place in water droplets.

For example, In above fig. we can see a flower in water droplets. This is due to the refraction of light. Sun flower get reflect from water droplets when light falls on it.

(6.) Refraction of light in river during sunset

In hilly area. This examples suit perfectly. But now, we will try to understand this example from above fig.

Enter Caption

During sunsets or sunrise. If we notice the activities of the rays of the sun in river. We will find the fringe pattern in river. like in above fig. This fringe pattern formed due to the refraction of light. This happens as: we know that light propagate in straight line. And During sunsets or sunrise, the rays of light strikes to the surface of the river parallely. Due to parallel touching to the the surface of the river, it gets bends in other direction. And this phenomena is happens not only with one rays of light. It is happens with many of the rays. And many of the rays refract in different-different direction. Due to this refraction, a shiny and fringe bright pattern formed on the surface of the river.

Refraction of light in river during sunset or sunrise can be understand in simple words. When a bundles of rays of light touches the upper surface of the river parallelly. It gets refract in many direction. And due to this diffraction. A fringe bright pattern formed. As shown in above fig.

(7.) Refraction in glass filled with water

Enter Caption

You can see a beautiful pattern in above fig. This pattern is formed due to the refraction of light. To know how? read further.

To understand this examples of refraction. we have to perform an experiment.

So lets take a glass. like normal tea glass.

Filled it half with water.

Darken a room by switched off all the bulbs. And close the doors and windows. So that there will be no any presence of light in the room.

Take a torch. Remember the torch should have straight light focus. And sure a white light torch.

Placed the glass filled with water in a white paper.

Light up the torch and adjust it in such a way that it focuses on the right middle of the glass. From upward direction.

Now, you can see the bright light pattern formed due to refraction.

Wants to know. How this bright pattern formed? So read the following last paragraph.

(8.) Refraction in diamond cut glass

Enter Caption

Diamond cut glass have been cutting in such a that when light enters in it. It refract again and again in inside automatically. So In diamond cut glass or even in diamond, a refraction of light takes place. We all noticed that a diamond is very shiny. And shows many color after passing a light beam through it.

This happens as: When a light beam enters into a diamond cut glass. Then that light beam do multiple reflection inside the diamond cut glass. And due to this multiple reflection. Diamond glow up. As shown in fig. During the passes of light wave inside the diamond cut glass. The light waves get bends due to the change in medium. And we know that refraction is the phenomena where medium changes. Hence, In diamond cut glass refraction occurs.

(9.) Rainbow is formed due to refraction

Enter Caption

Refraction is the causes of the formation of rainbow. This sounds very wired. Because till now we studied that formation of rainbow is due to the diffraction of light. So I will tell you Both the phenomena are responsible for the formation of rainbow. Know how?

In rainy season, clouds are present in the atmosphere. And when a light beam touches the cloud. then some of the light waves get diffract in different direction and some are passed through the cloud. And those light which passed through cloud, is also responsible for the formation of rainbow.

Fore more details on the formation of rainbow through diffraction. click here.

(10.) Refraction of light in our eye lens

Refraction also happens in our eyes. So eye is also an example of refraction of light. We call eye but that's doesn't mean the whole eye. Refraction occurs only in our eye lens. Our eye has a convex lens. So when we see things the light from the emitting source hits the object and then light wave come into our eyes. And when light enters in our eyes through eye lens called 'convex lens' the light get bends and falls in our retina. where inverted image formed. After that our mind re-correct the image through brain nerves system. We already discussed about refraction phenomena in convex lens in detail. Look first examples of refraction of light. we also provide the information about refraction in concave lens.

As refraction occurs in convex lens. On the same way refraction occurs in our eye.

Application of refraction of light in daily life

Refraction of light can be seen in measuring scale.

Microscope works on the application of refraction of light.

Refraction is used in working telescope.

Our eye works on the application of refraction of light.

Eye contact lens works on the principal of refraction of light.

Want more in detail explanation of application of refraction of light. then click the link.

Q&A on Refraction of light

1. Where does refraction occurs in the human eyes?

Ans:- Refraction of light occurs on the eye lens of the human eyes. This happens as follows, when a beam of light enters through eyeball it pass though eye lens that is convex lens and refraction of light takes place.

2. How is a camera an example of refraction?

Ans:- camera is the best example of refraction of light. How? See in camera there is a lens placed on the top front part of the camera. From where photographer see the images and click photos. Now let's understand how does camera use refraction? So this happens as follows: when we see an image though the camera lens placed on the top front part of the camera. The rays of light coming from the image enter through those camera lens and refraction occurs in camera.

Please note that convex lens is used in camera lens.

3. Is a shadow reflection or refraction?

Ans:- shadow is neither a reflection or refraction of light. It is the dark area where light not reach. In other words you can say a shadow is the region where there is no light beam. A shadow is formed when an object or body come in the path of a straight travelling ligh beam. Then a dark image of that object or body formed as similar vto their shape and size and we call them a shadow.

4. Is flashlight reflection or refraction?

Ans:- A flashlight is an example of reflection of light. Because a flashlight works as quite similar as a torch works. As we know in a torch thee is a shiny polished silver like plastic placed in the back part of the bulb. And bulb placed at the focus point.

XI

Difference Between Reflection and Refraction

Reflection and refraction both are the concept holder of optics. In optics both have a different laws. i.e, Laws of reflection and laws of refraction. Basically these laws are the back bone of optics or light. 50% of the syllabus of optics hold by these two laws. So before we procced to find the differences and similarities between reflection and refraction of light. We should have to know a little about reflection and refraction.

Concept of Reflection in optics

In simple word, reflection is the bouncing back of light. That means, In reflection of light, light waves get reflect when falls on a surface. weather it is smooth or rough. For smooth surface it follows the law of reflection of light but for rough surface it gets diffuse and don't follow the law of reflection of light.

Law of reflection of light:-

Incident ray, the reflected ray, Normal and the point of incident where incident ray touches the surface, all lies on the same plane lines.

When a beam of light falls on a smooth surface obliquely, it gets reflect in the same direction with making an equal angle to the normal lines. i.e, Incident ray makes angle $\angle i$ with the normal whereas reflected ray makes angle $\angle r$ with the normal. And both the angles $\angle i$ and $\angle r$ becomes equal to each other.

Hence, In law of reflection of light ∠i = ∠r. Please note that reflection of light occurs only when light travels in one medium.

Refraction of light:-

In simple word, refraction of light is the bending of light, when travelling from one medium to another medium. That means, when a beam of light passing through another medium (which have different refractive index to the compare of first medium) then, it gets bend at the edge of the second medium.

Refraction of light also have two laws.

An incident ray, the refracted ray, the point of incidence and Normal all lies on the same plane.

When a beam of light falls obliquely on a second medium, it gets bend through the edge of that medium. Because, when light strikes at the edge their velocity get changes due to this it get refract in another direction. So thats the reason where sine angle of incidence to the sine angle of refraction always be constant.

Hence, the law of refraction has sine ∠i to the sine angle ∠r is constant. or sine ∠i / sine ∠r = constant.

Here following are the 7 key differences and similarities between reflection and refraction of light. All the given differences and similarities are explained in detail. In further part of this post.

7 key differences and similarities between reflection and refraction of light

(1.) Reflection is the bouncing back of light when falls on a smooth surface(or any other surface). On the other hand refraction is the banding of light when falls on the surface of the medium.

(2.) Reflection of light takes place in only one medium but refraction of light takes place in two different medium.

(3.) During the reflection, speed of light remains same but during refraction speed of light changes (increases or decreases).

(4.) In reflection of light the angle of incidence is equal to the angle of refraction. While In refraction of light the angle of incidence is not equal to the angle of refraction.

(5.) In reflection of light, the incidence ray, the reflected ray, the normal and the point of incidence lies on the same plane. Similarly In refraction of light, the incidence ray, the refracted ray, the normal and the point of incidence lies on the same plane.

(6.) In reflection of light the one sided of the medium must be polished. But In refraction both the side of the medium must be transparent.

(7.) In reflection there are total two laws. Similarly, In refraction there are also two laws.

XII

Diffraction of light

What is Diffraction of light?

When an obstacle or aperture is in the path of a wave, the wave bends around the corners of the obstacle or aperture. This bending of wave around the corners of an obstacle or aperture is called diffraction.

All waves exhibit the phenomenon of diffraction. Diffraction effects occur with longitudinal as well as transverse waves.

Diffraction of light

The phenomenon of bending of light wave around the corners of an obstacle or aperture is called diffraction of light.

Due to the bending of light around the corners of an obstacle or aperture, the light deviates from its straight line path and enters into the geometrical shadow of the obstacle. The bending or diffraction of light becomes much more pronounced when the size of the obstacle or aperture is comparable to the wavelength of light. thus the smaller the size of the aperture, the greater is the bending of light around the corners of the obstacle or aperture and vice-versa.

Enter Caption

According to Huygen's principle, the aperture acts as a new source of secondary wavelets.

The following points are worth noting about the diffraction of light.

Diffraction of light is not easily noticed because the obstacles and the apertures of the size of wavelength of light 10 to the power -6.

In ray optics, we ignore diffraction and assume that light travels in straight lines. this assumption is responsible because under ordinary conditions, diffraction of light is negligible.

The smaller the size of the obstacle the greater the bending of light around the corners and vice-versa.

Top 10 examples of diffraction of light in everyday life.

Laser light shows diffraction by using blade

Ring around moon due to diffraction on water droplets
Diffraction of light by telescope
Diffraction of light by optical instrument
Diffraction of light in CD or DVD disk
Diffraction of light in Measure scale
Diffraction of light in diamond cut glass
Diffraction of light in Sky after rain
Diffraction of light in book hologram
Diffraction of light to form shadow of an object
Diffraction by bending of light at the corner edge of an object
Rainbow is formed due to diffraction

To understand these examples of diffraction of light in more detailed then read further. below are the full explanation of all the examples of diffraction of light in detail.

Types of Diffraction

The diffraction phenomenon is generally divided into the following two classes:

Fraunhofer's diffraction:- This type of diffraction takes place at a narrow slit when parallel rays of light (or plane wavefront) are incident on it. clearly both the source and the screen should be at infinite distance from the narrow slit. To obtain Fraunhofer's diffraction in the laboratory, we use a conversing lens.

Note:- you can understand it by taking an example of Young's Double slit experiment. this experiment shows that how a narrow slit diffract a light wave or plane wavefront and fall on a screen and formed a fringe width.

Fresnel's diffraction:- This type of diffraction takes place at a narrow slit when non-parallel rays of light are incident on it. In this case, the source of light is close to the slit so that the wavefront is either spherical or cylindrical. the screen is also at a finite distance from the slit. Fresnel's diffraction is rather complex to treat quantitatively.

examples of diffraction of light in everyday life

In our day to day life, we observe many natural phenomenon. like formation of rainbow after heavy rain, formation of seven colour when light pass through curve glass, glowing of DVD disk when viewed by some angle etc. but we are not so curious about to know how this phenomenon happens. or what's the reason behind this. So today, we will discuss about such natural phenomenon that happens with us in our daily life, but we ignore that.

1. laser light shows diffraction by using blade

In their life, every one used laser light. but do you know laser light shows diffraction of light after passing through two blade. If blades are arrange in such a way that the edge gap between the blades are narrow slit then passing light through that slit shows diffraction of light.

This experiment is same as Young's double slit experiment. If you do not understood this laser light experiment then take a look on the below video, you will understand.

2. Ring around moon due to diffraction on water droplets

Everyday there are many natural phenomenon happen on earth as well as in universe. some of them are observed by human some are not. but we are not so curious to know the reason behind that phenomenon. formation of ring around the moon is one of them natural phenomenon. which look amazing. but how they happens. so lets know the reason behind this phenomenon.

Formation of ring around moon is due to the diffraction of light. this types of diffraction occur once in a long time. this happens as when sun, earth and moon comes in a straight line then the moon covers the whole sun for some times and due to diffraction of light coming from the sun bends around the moon's edge and a ring formation is like to occur when seen from the earth.

3. Diffraction of light by telescope

telescope shows diffraction of light. when we see any objects from telescope then telescope forms image of an object which we see in the form of point source which is coming from the object and these point sources collect in the focal plane of the telescope. these point image is created by wave interference around the the focal point. due to the diffraction of light the point sources produces various interference or diffraction in the image formed in the telescope.

4. Diffraction of light by optical instrument

In optical instrument like telescope, Microscope, camera lenses etc. shows diffraction of light. camera lens are the best examples of diffraction of light in our daily life. we can easily observe the diffraction pattern in camera lenses. After viewing the camera lenses from some angle in bright sunlight, diffraction of light can easily observed.

5. Diffraction of light in CD or DVD disk

In day to day life we all must saw the CD or DVD disk, and also played with them. but many of us can't notice one physics phenomenon that happens on CD or DVD disk. If we see the CD disk from some angle in bright light then we saw a rainbow pattern on the polished side of the DVD disk. that pattern of colours are due to diffraction of light.

In CD or DVD disk, there are many small peaces of narrow chip placed in the polished side of the disk. this narrow chip stores the data. and made up of thin plane shiny sheets. When a ray of light falls on that part of the disk, the disk appears like rainbow. due to the diffraction of light.

6. Diffraction of light in Measure scale

every student in their life must be use a scale in childhood. If we notice that scale scattering a white light into seven colour. many of the student play with them and become happy, when they seen a rainbow on their scale. I am also played with them.???.

But what the reason behind that scattering of light phenomenon. we should curious about to know that, but we don't.

The reason behind the formation of rainbow on measuring scale is due to the diffraction of light. (or refraction of light). this happens as when a beam of white light falls on the edge of measuring scale then it's edge scattering that white light into seven colour and the formation of rainbow takes place.

7. Diffraction of light in diamond cut glass

everyone saw a diamond cut glass in their life. diamond cut glass are used in decorative items. If we see any decorative items having a diamond cut glass on it, then we will notice that when sunlight or other source of light falls on the the glass it diffract light to the another way and formed seven colour like rainbow.

But everyone have a doubt that How this phenomenon of diffraction of light happens in diamond cut glass? so lets understand it. even it is very simple. the same principle works on it as in the glass prism. we know that a glass prism scattering a white light into seven colour due to the diffraction of light. In the same way white light diffract in the diamond cut glass.

8. Diffraction of light in Sky after rain

In rainy season we are waiting to see the rainbow. but, how rainbow is formed? a simplest asked question by many people. so the reason behind the formation of rainbow is due to the scattering of white light into seven colour.

Rainbow is formed due to the diffraction of white light in the sky in some cases. this happens as, In rainy season the water droplets are present in the sky. the water droplets are in the shape of spherical and when a beam of white light falls on the water droplets it diffract the light in the sky and formation of rainbow takes place.

FAQ on examples of diffraction of light in everyday life

What are some examples of diffraction?

Diffraction of light in book hologram.

Diffraction of light to form shadow of an object.

Diffraction by bending of light at the corner edge of an object.

Rainbow is formed due to diffraction.

Is a rainbow An example of diffraction?

The actual meaning of diffraction is the interference of light wave passed through a slit and form a fringe when falls on a screen. Rainbow formation works on the principal of refraction of light. Not diffraction of light. But in some cases diffraction of light is responsible for formation of rainbow.

What are the two types of diffraction?

The diffraction phenomenon is generally divided into the following two classes:

Fraunhofer's diffraction:- This type of diffraction takes place at a narrow slit when parallel rays of light (or plane wavefront) are incident on it.

Fresnel's diffraction:- This type of diffraction takes place at a narrow slit when non-parallel rays of light are incident on it.

XIII

Application of Refraction

5 Applications of refraction of light in daily life

Refraction of light can be seen in measuring scale.

Microscope works on the application of refraction of light.

Refraction is used in working telescope.

Our eye works on the application of refraction of light.

Eye contact lens works on the application of refraction.

Now, we try to understand all the above applications of refraction of light in detail one by one.

(1.) Refraction of light in measuring scale

In our student life we have used measuring scale. And at that time everyone must observe one thing. When we tried to see through the measuring scale, we noticed the formation of some colorful pattern in scale. So what was that pattern? And Why formed? The answer is that pattern was due to the light entering in the measuring scale. And they formed due to the refraction of light. Know how?

When light falls on our eyes passing through the measuring scale. It get refract or bend at the edge of the measuring scale. Because light is coming from air (medium 1) and then get enters into measuring scale (medium 2). And we studied that when light enters from one medium to another medium, it gets bends. So due to the change in medium, the speed of light get decreases, And colorful pattern formed.

(2.) Microscope works on the refraction

We all see the microscope in our school laboratory. If we noticed that there is some small lenses fitted in microscope. So what is that lens? And what is their work? So before answering all these questions, we have to know about microscope.

A microscope is an instrument through which we can see micro-organism, bacteria, viruses etc. which is not possible to see from our naked eyes.

The lenses used in microscope to see micro-organism is convex lens. That lens magnifies the object so that it appears bigger than original size.

When we try to see through microscope, the light coming from outside get enters in our eyes through these lenses. Hence, we can say that the refraction of light takes place in microscope.

(3.) Refraction in working telescope

In telescope there is also presence of lenses. We use telescope to see starts and the behaviour of the planets. Scientist also use telescope to notice the position of stars and planets. Please note that telescope is just quite similar to microscope.

Telescope also works on the application of refraction of light. This happens as follows: When we see stars and planet through telescope. The lenses present in it get refract the light coming from stars and planet and bend it through some angles. So that the stars and planets looks closer to our eyes.

(4.) Eye works on the application of refraction of light

Apart from microscope and telescope. Human eyes are also works on the application of refraction of light. This is because of the presence of convex lenses in our eyes. Convex lenses refract or bend the light wave coming from outside and divert it in our retina. So retina forms images which is inverted. But our mind rearrange that image.

Our eye are the best application of refraction of light.

(5.) Eye contact lens works on the application of refraction

Those people who have not clear vision. They uses eye contact lenses for clear view. So what is that lens made up of? That lenses are convex lens.

Those person who has weak sightedness. They wears eye contact lens because as we know that convex lenses are used in eye contact glass. So it helps to refract the light.

XIV

Relation between force and Potential energy

Introduction

After the discussion of physics, chemistry, mathematics in approx 200 posts. Now after a long break, we have planed to discuss physics. Now a day, a more simple question is trending on the internet that is what is the main relation or co-relation between force and potential energy. So the answer is available but not in simple word. So here we have establish a relation between force and potential energy in simplest word. even a 10th student can understand it well.

So before any wasting of time lets start. But before we start, lets take an overview on the concept of force and potential energy.

We have already studied that when we talk about the term potential energy ie, we are actually talking about conservative forces. Because we have already studied in our previous classes that in case of Non-conservative forces, no storage of energy is possible. Full work done or whole amount of work done is concerned in terms of energy loss.

Whenever we talk about potential or stored form of energy that actually means we are talking about conservative forces. And in case of conservative forces, work done is always form of potential energy. Here what is work done means? The answer is work done is nothing but a change in potential energy.

> "*Please not that the whole concept of this relation of force and potential energy is only that "**work done is equal to the change in potential energy**".*"

Work done = Change in potential energy

$\Delta W = \Delta U2 - \Delta U1$

$\therefore \Delta W = \Delta U$

From the above short discussion, we have concluded that the relation between force and potential energy is work done with change in potential energy.

Before we discuss the relation with examples and graph. lets first understand some terms which is used here. like what is the meaning of force, conservative force, Potential energy etc.

What is Force in terms of conservative force?

If we not see the concept of conservative. Then we can define force as simple, a push or a pull of an object is called force. In other words, if a body experience some changes in its state wether it is in motion or rest. Then there must be something acted upon the body called force.

Now, let's define force in terms of conservative force. So, a conservative force is like a gravitational force that acted between two bodies having some masses. For example, gravitational force always acting between the earth and any other mass bodies.

For better understanding in conservative force. Always remember, those forces which acted on potential energy know as conservative force.

Conservative force always determined only when, when there will be the final displacement of the object in potential energy.

In simple words, conservative force helps in work done only when, there will be some changes in the position of the object.

Means the work done by conservative force not dependent on path.

Mathematical concepts of conservative force

The term Conservative force comes from Stored energy concept. Means conservative force comes from the concept of mechanical energy.

The most common conservative force are gravity and spring forces (also known as stored energy force).

What is potential energy in terms of conservative force?

Potential energy is a type of stored energy. If we decine potential energy in terms of conservative force. Then definition will be like, When work is done by the displacement of an object from initial to final position due to the conservative force known as potential energy.

You can consider gravitation force to understand the concept of potential energy.

Now, take a look for what you are expected from this post. i.e, the relationship between force and potential energy.

Establish a relation between force and potential energy.

Let's take an example to establish a relation and co relation between force (or conservative force) and potential energy.

Take a conservative field, and divide it into two parts (may or may not be equal). Mark a point A in the left part and point B in the right part. As shown in fig.

Suppose when a body is in a side of point A, then its energy is U^1 and when it is in side of point B, it's energy is U^2. Please note that it is given ($U^1 > U^2$). This shows that body A has more energy than body B.

We all know that every body has a tendency to achieve the minimum energy state. So, in this case body at point B has less energy. Therefore, body at point A transfer the energy to the body B. And when body A releases the energy towards body B, then the conservative field will exert a conservative force towards the direction of energy flow.

Now, when a work is done to being body A to the body B by the force (F), then change kar n work done will be equal to the change in potential energy.

I.e,

$\Delta W = UA - UB$

$\Delta W = f. dx$

Similarly,

In the above example, when we bought a body A towards the body B, then potential energy of body A decreases and due to this the potential energy of the body B increases.

That meas to do work done, change in potential energy takes place.

Therefore,

$\Delta W = - \Delta U$

Here, minus sign indicates that the energy is decreasing.

The same thing happens when being body A towards body B but in step by step. I.e, to cover less amount of distance. The result of work done will be as equal to happen in above case.

Let suppose A and B are located at on x axis. And potential energy of a body is given as two function of position at every point where potential energy is changing.

So, when the body is going from one point to another point say A to B.

We can state the above example as, in displacing the body by dx, let dU be the decreasing in P.E of the system. Then we can use

$- dU = F. dx$

Because by displacing from point A to B by dx. The work done by force (F) is F. dx.

We can write:-

$dU = - F. dx$

Or,

$F = -dU / dx$

This relation is well at for undirectional varient in P.E.

Please note that :- The minus sign always shows that the force acting in the direction where potential energy is decreasing.

Here, we have discussed only about one dimensional system. But when potential energy acts on two dimension or three dimensions (or free space). Then what will happen. Let's take a look.

In free space or three dimensions variation of P.E. we use,

$F = - \Delta U = -$ gradient of U.

Here, delta is gradient oprator.

Hence, the required relation between force and potential energy is

$F = - \Delta U.$

For getting above photo scan this QR code in your anroid scanner. You can download web scanner from play store.

Sciencelaws.in

XV

Explain potential difference, work done and charge moved

State relation between Potential difference, work done and charge moved

Potential difference, work done and charge moved. You have heard these words in class 9. If you have remembered that there were a formula related there words. We can also say that formula as the relation between potential difference, work done and charge moved.

In this post we will discuss about this relationship in more details. But before we proceed we have to clear our doubt about these terms. Potential difference, work done and charge moved.

So firstly we will define potential difference then work done and charge moved. After the definition of all these terms, we will state the relation between them. And to prove our relation we will also establish the derivation of that relation. So let's t with potential difference.

What is potential difference?

Potential difference is defined as the amount of work done to bring a unit charge from one position to another position.

In other words, potential difference is the difference of charges between two points because of the movement of change from first point to second point.

Let's suppose there are two point charge q^1 and q^2. Separated by the distance 'r'. Both the charges applying forces to each other weather it is repulsive or attractive.

<u>Case 1:-</u> (q^1>q^2)

Let's suppose the force act on both the charges be repulsive. Due to this one chance q^1 applyed more force to q^2. So that q^2 moved away from q^1. Now the distance between both charges will be (r+1).

The potential difference between both the charges will be

Potential difference = work done / charge.

<u>Case 2:-</u> (q^1<q^2)

In this case q^2 is greater than q^1. So that q^2 acquire more forces to the compare of q^1. Let's suppose q^1 and q^2 both are positive charges. S

Hence, here is also a repulsive force acts on each other. So due to the repulsive force q^1 get far away from q^2. Therefore the distance between both the charges will be r+1.

Here the formula of potential difference will be same as above

Potential difference = work done / charge.

S.I unit of Potential Difference is Volt.

To know more about potential difference. click here because here you can also know there is a direct <u>connection of potential difference with ohm's law</u>.

What is work done?

Work done is defined as the when we apply a force on something and body get displaced from its initial position then work is said to be done.

In other words work is said to be done when we apply a force 'F' on some body or object and body get displaced from its initial positions. If force is apply but body didn't get displaced from its initial position then work is not said to be done.

These are the some conditions that we have must follow for work done.

- force not should be zero.
- Body must cover some distance after force applied.
- Displacement should not be zero.

The formula for calculating work done is given by,

Work Done = force . Displacement

State the relation between potential difference, work done and charge moved

The main relation between potential difference, work done and charge moved is potential difference is always equal to the amount of work done per unit charge. Hence, the mathematical relation between potential difference, work done and charge moved will be,

Potential difference = work done / charge moved

lets understand this relation with the help of an example. suppose we have two charged bodies q and Q placed at the position A and B respectively. Both the body have 1 coulomb of charge in it. Now, If we bring the charge 'Q' to the charge 'q' then we have to do some work. So, in that case how much the amount of work will be done with respect of bringing charged is said to be potential difference.

Because of the movement of charge from one position to another position there must be the unbalanced quantity of charge. means when we brought the charge 'Q' to the charge 'q'. then the position B which had charge 'Q' will have loss of charge. but at position A. there will be gain of charge.

So Due to the loss or gain of charge between two points. There should be the difference in charge known as potential difference.

As we discussed above that when force applied and something start moving then work is done. hence, work will also done in the above case because we apply the force on charge Q and after force applied it started moving.

So, here work done with respect to the amount of charge we want to move. But as we discussed above that there are only 1 coulomb of charge on both the points A and B. So, the total work done will be the respect of 1 coulomb of charge. Suppose in the above case the total work done is W.

Therefore, potential difference will be equal to the W / 1 coulomb charge.

Potential Difference = W / C

Drive the relation between potential difference, work done and charge moved

As we above established the relation between potential difference, work done and charge moved is given by,

Potential Difference = work done / charge moved ---------------------- (1)

Now, lets drive the above equation.

If we define 1 Volt of potential difference then we can easily get the formula of the relation between potential difference, work done and charge moved.

1 Volt of potential difference is defined as the when 1 joule of work is done to bring a 1 coulomb of charge from one point to another point where the another charge situated then 1 Volt of potential difference generated between these two charges.

1 Volt = 1 Joule / 1 coulomb

Potential Difference = Work done / moved charge

We can also drive it with another method but this could be the simplest method. that is easy to understand.

XVI

Relation between frequency and wavelength

The main relation between frequency and wavelength is frequency is inversely proportional to the wavelength. that means if frequency of the wave increases then wavelength decreases and if the frequency decreases then wavelength increases. that is given by,

$f \propto 1/\lambda$

Hence, the formula of relation between frequency and wavelength is $f \propto 1/\lambda$.

Now, as we know that the relation between frequency and wavelength is frequency is inversely proportional to the wavelength. but we have to deep analysis about frequency and wavelength. we should also know about How frequency and wavelength are related to each other? so In this article we discussed more about frequency and wavelength in the later below. and also we solve derivation of relation between frequency and wavelength.

Wavelength

The minimum distance in which a sound wave repeats itself is called its wavelength. In most simple words, it is the length of one complete wave. It is denoted by λ . In a sound wave, the combined length of a compression and an adjacent rarefaction is called its wavelength. In a sound wave, the distance between the center of two consecutive compression and two consecutive rarefaction is also called its wavelength. S.I unit of wavelength is meter (m).

Please note that the distance between the center of a compression and an adjacent rarefaction is equal to the half of the wavelength. $\lambda/2$.

Frequency

The term frequency tells us the rate at which the waves are produced by their source. in other words frequency is the number of cycles produced in one second is called the frequency of the wave. Since the one complete wave is produced by one full vibration of the vibrating body, so we can say that the number of vibration per second is also called frequency of the wave. it is denoted by f. S.I unit of frequency is Hertz (Hz).

Derivation of relation between frequency and wavelength.

for a given light wave,

Distance = Speed × Time

Speed (Velocity) = Distance travcled by wave / Time period

Velocity of light = Wavelength/ Time period

$V = \lambda/T$

$V = \lambda \times 1/T$

$V = \lambda \times f \because [1/T = f]$

or, $\mathbf{f \propto 1/\lambda}$,

we can say that **the relation between frequency and wavelength is $f \propto 1/\lambda$.**

relation between frequency and wavelength explain in detailed

Imagine a beam of light wave travels in a medium with very small velocity. (assume speed of light is less than 3 × 10^8 m/s). So according to our imagination, light beam looks like this,

So in this case frequency of the light wave is very small due to low velocity. Now imagine the velocity of the light goes faster, more faster, even more faster. Then the beam of light wave looks like this,

we observed from this experiment that as speed of light increases the wave becomes more curve. That means the amplitude of the wave increases. So, we can say that after increasing the velocity of the light wave, the number of cycles of the wave increases and amplitude of wave also increases. i.e, frequency is directly proportional to the velocity of the light wave and velocity is directly proportional to the amplitude of the light wave. that is given by,

Frequency ∝ velocity ∝ Amplitude

Now after looking deep in the second experiment, we will observe that the all three waves say something. That is if we calculate the length of the first wave, the second wave and the third wave. We will find that the as we increases the speed of light wave the length of the wave decreases. i.e, if we compare the first wave and third wave in second experiment we will notice that the length of the third wave is smaller than that of the first wave due to the increase in velocity of the wave.

Conclusion

so we conclude that after increasing in velocity of the wave the wavelength decrease. But frequency increases. therefore the relation between frequency, wavelength and velocity is, **Frequency ∝ velocity ∝ 1/wavelength. That means frequency is inversely proportional to the wavelength but directly proportional to the velocity of the wave.**

Relation between frequency, wavelength, and velocity:-

If we increase the velocity of the wave then frequency also increases but wavelength of the wve decreases.

Distance = speed

Distance = Speed × Time

Speed (Velocity) = Distance traveled by wave / Time period

Velocity of light = Wavelength/ Time period

$V = \lambda/T$

$V= \lambda \times 1/T$

$\mathbf{V = \lambda \times f}$

Hence, the relation between frequency, velocity and wavelength is $V = \lambda \times f$.

<u>Also Read</u>

FAQ on relation between frequency and wavelength

Are wavelength and frequency directly or inversely related?

wavelength and frequency is inversely proportional to each other. i.e, $f \propto 1/\lambda$.

What is the relation between speed of sound frequency and wavelength?

the relation between speed of sound frequency and wavelength is $V = \lambda \times f$.

Is frequency directly proportional to wavelength?

No,frequency is inversely proportional to wavelength.

What happens to wavelength as frequency increases?

When frequency increases then wavelength decreases.

XVII
Wonders of Science

Please note that this essay on wonders of science is about 500 words to 1000 words. Student can also use this essay. If they are in class 9th, 10th and 12th. Remember this essay is for senior students.

Introduction to wonders of science

There are many wonders of science in the world. Even this phone is one of the wonders of science and technology. In this new era, technology is growing by leap and bound. Today if we sit to count the wonders of science, I think it may take our whole day but counting will never stop. So Whenever there is the presence of science and technology, the wonders will always happen.

Our earth has infinite natural phenomena even that till science cannot understand it completely. But apart from all the mysteries. There are some common wonders of science that if it would not invented then life has not become so easy. These are:

1. Means of communication
2. Means of Transportation
3. Means of Electricity
4. Computer
5. Medical

Lets understand all these wonders of science one by one in detail. All the given wonders of science has explained in detail on another post of this website. link to go there to read full article.

(1.) Means of communication:-

means of communication is one of the important wonders of science. Tv, Radio, Newspaper, mobile, these are the means of communication. internet and telegram is the fastest means of communication.

(2.) Means of Transportation

Means of transportation are car, bus train, flight etc. it is one of the best wonders of science. we can travels from one place to another place by train, bus, flight etc. these all are the wonders of science. science plays an important role in our life from the past years. without science we can't imagine our life. transportation is one of the important inventions of science.

(3.) Means of electricity

In the modern time electricity is an important source of energy. electricity is used in various field like in our home for glowing bulbs, fans, motor, and many more appliances. In factories, In transport etc. without electricity we can't imagine our life. electricity is very important invention of science. all the inventions took place depends on electricity.

(4.) Computer

computer is most famous wonders ofscience. it is the greatest invention in science and technology. it is the fastest machine till now.Now a day many of the complicated word done by computer very easily and comfortably, that's why computer is used everywhere like in offices, schools, labs, railway, airport, hospital etc.

(5.) Medical

science has prevent human beings by many diseases. it has made us healthier. In the age of science it is possible to transplant any organ of body.

These are the topics of wonder of modern science composition:-

- Science in the service of humanity.

- Science in human life.

- Science uses and abuse.

- Science and human.

- Science in our daily life.

- Science in a good service but bad master.

- Science a boon or a curse.

- Science and technology.

wonders of science essay for class 10th

This is absolutely true that science is wonder. Without science we didn't expects our life. Now a day science becomes our parts of daily life. We all covered with science and technology. Even our environment too. But there are some special wonders of science that if it didn't then our life will not be like this today. Today we use phones, electric vehicles, motor, computer etc just because of science. But there are some common inventions in the past that if it didn't invented then this all technology which we have right now, was not possible. So, given are the list of wonders of science.

- Electricity
- Advantage of science
- Disadvantage of science
- Means of Computer
- Agriculture
- Modern devices
- Internet
- Social media
- Space technology
- Conclusion

XVIII
Science and Technology - 1

wonders of science essay in 150 words.

There are many wonders of science in the world. even this is not wrong if we say science is itself a wonder, but the most wonder is our universe. a lot of wonders of science is present in our universe. like our earth is one of them. there are many wonders of science present on the earth. like our technology is one of the wonders of science.

we can communicate with each other, we can travels from one place to another place by train, bus, flight etc. these all are the wonders of science. science plays an important role in our life from the past years. without science we can't imagine our life.

Now we have modern technology, we can do all things which is not possible in early age like we can go in outer space, we can communicate with other people by video calling, we can save our earth by any types of space problems. we can do all these things just because of science. science gave us a wonderful life.

Wonders of science ka nibandh

Introduction

Inventions of science

Means of communication

Means of electricity

Means of transportation

computer

Medical science

Disadvantage of science

Conclusion

Wonders of science Introduction

It is the world of science. science has given us many wonders till now from the early age. It made impossible things possible like we can communicate with other people no matter how far the distance is. basically it plays an important role in our life. without science we can't imagine life. without science we can't develop. so we can say that our life becomes easier and reliable just because of science, but what is the actual meaning of science?

the answer is science is nothing but it is systematic knowledge of anything like laws, experiment, theories, principle etc.

one of the most famous wonders of science is electricity. In the modern time electricity is an important source of energy. electricity is used in various field like in our home for glowing bulbs, fans, motor, and many more appliances. In factories, In transport etc. without electricity we can't imagine our life.

wonders of science and inventions

wonders of science and inventions. there are many inventions done by scientist from the past years till now. many of the inventions are done just accidentally during experiment. Now we have a lot of technology due to science, but without inventions we haven't any technology. we can communicate, we can travel from one place to another no matter how far the distance is, we can cover it within hours just because of inventions. In this age we have many big and small inventions. that's why we can live a comfortable and easier life. we have electricity, computer, Radio, camera, phone, Washing machine, Ac, cooler, and many things.

Means of communication (wonders of science)

means of communication is one of the important wonders of science. Tv, Radio, Newspaper, mobile, these are the means of communication. internet and telegram is the fastest means of communication. at present we can communicate with the whole world. we can communicate with other people by video calling, we can communicate by messaging. In early age people communicate with each other by letter so it took a lot of time but now a day we can communicate in a second to any person no matter how far is he from our place. We can also sand our information, our thought to the whole world by social media. social media now becomes a greatest communication platform to communicate and send message quickly.

Means of electricity (wonders of science).

one of the most famous wonders of science is electricity. In the modern time electricity is an important source of energy. electricity is used in various field like in our home for glowing bulbs, fans, motor, and many more appliances. In factories, In transport etc. without electricity we can't imagine our life. electricity is very important invention of science. all the inventions took place depends on electricity. so we can say that electricity is one of the important inventions in science and it is one of the wonders of science.

Means of transportation (wonders of science)

means of transportation are car, bus train, flight etc. it is one of the best wonders of science. we can travels from one place to another place by train, bus, flight etc. these all are the wonders of science. science plays an important role in our life from the past years. without science we can't imagine our life. transportation is one of the important inventions of science. human beings can reach any part of the earth, this is not wrong if we say human can reach any part of the universe but not now, may be in future. science may be develop on that level so man can reach any part of the universe. man reached even in other planets.

wonders of science computer

computer is most famous wonders of science. it is the greatest invention in science and technology. it is the fastest machine till now.Now a day many of the complicated word done by computer very easily and comfortably, that's why computer is used everywhere like in offices, schools, labs, railway, airport, hospital etc. it is widely used machine because it can do hard and hard work very easily for example it can calculate a large and complicated number very easily. we are talking about computer so this will be wrong if we cant say about charles Babbage the inventor of first computer. the first computer can only calculate the number that's it. but it can took a room size place for operate.

Medical science (wonders of science)

science has prevent human beings by many diseases. it has made us healthier. In the age of science it is possible to transplant any organ of body. science can control all types of Incurable diseases like T.B, cancer etc. it has given eye to the blind persons.

Disadvantage of science

Everything has two aspects. in the same way science has also dark side. Atom bombs and other dangerous weapons. these weapons can destroy human beings as well as our earth.

Conclusion

we can say that science is good servant but bad master. if we use science in good direction then it can change our life and makes heaven, but if we use it in wrong way then it curse in our life. it totally depends on us that how we can address science and his dangerous inventions like hydrogen bombs, Nuclear bombs etc.

XIX

Science in Everyday life

science in everyday life essay 350 words

"Science in everyday life" This line is absolutely right because science is everywhere and anywhere. you have to just look carefully and observe it carefully. Without science nothing exist. If you see anything happens around you like miracle there is science. In actual that was not miracle that's behinds science. we can easily say that our everyday life consist of many scientific process. everyday we do many things and daily stuff like sleeping, Bathing, Dancing, playing, Walking, running, and much more. they all have science and scientific reason behind them but we have to look then carefully and observe them carefully.

If we look around in our environment there are lot of science and scientific process behind them but we can't observe them by our simple looking. we have to carefully observe them. many of the thing happens in our life or we can say science in everyday life, some examples are given below to illustrate the science in everyday life so lets start.

science in everyday life examples, If we are in our room there is all around wall this is a simple looking, but if we observe the wall carefully then the wall is made up of small particles called atom or molecules this is scientific observation. If we look around in our environment there are many things happen like in rainy season the lighting of thunder, formation of rainbow, sound of thunder and much more things.

If we observe our daily work we do there's a lot of science let see how science covered our whole life.

we woke up in the morning, we saw sun rises in the east, here is science, how? the answer is sun rises in the east this is universal truth sun always rise in the direction of east and sun set in the west because our earth revolve to the direction of west to east so sun rises in the east and set in west. If we take bath and we apply soap or detergent powder on our cloth, we feel some hotness when rub detergent on our hand because of scientific reason. soap and detergent contains sodium molecules in it which feel warm when rub in hand.

science in everyday life essay 150 words

science in everyday life Now a day science becomes important for human beings. but In early era human needs food, shelter, and cloth for their survival. they faces many problems but overcomes them and become civilized man with the help of science. Now science becomes a way of life.

early man kills the animals and eat food for their survival. they first discovered fire, they took two stones and strike them and invent fire.

Now scientist observe many things happen in our environment they want to know why and how things happen in our universe. they follow the process of discovery and make rules. and we follow them by reading in books in the form of laws and theories. so we can say that early man is our first scientist. Now a day many things depend upon technology and technology comes with the help of science. our life totally depends on science so we can say that science exist in everyday life. for example we read this essay on phone which is a technology and we all know that technology come with science.

XX

Science And Technology

here you find science and technology essay in 150 words, 250 words, 300 words, 500 words.

science and technology essay these two words are the backbone of development of Earth. Technology is not complete without science.

They both are interconnected. Now a days our society, our country, our whole Earth is developing very fast in the field of technology just because of science.This is not wrong at all if I said science is our life and science is everywhere. If you look around where you stand you can see many stuff around you which carries science and science laws inside itself.

If you see any natural cause around you like common cause raining, lightning, sunrise, sun set a general observation on earth carried out science laws and scientific reasons. I can just say that this is an endless topic (science and technology). This can never be end and not complete all the science laws and scientific reasons in any long article or essay, but you have a proper and different knowledge about science and technology.

So I will try to cover more and more clarity about science and technology in just a few words so you can write an essay in easy way in a few words and your intention will be fulfilled to come to this website.where you find all the possible science theories and all the practical science laws as possible.
Hi my name is Aditya Raj Anand so let's start.

science and technology both are the widely used words. Everyone heard about that in his or her life. Science and technology both are just as twins brother or we can say one soul two bodies hahaha.
Science is world and world is science.

you can also say that, actually we covered with science and technology. our life depend on science and technology. we can't imagine life without science and technology. it is very difficult now to spend life without science and technology. science and technology plays very important role in our life. we woke up in the morning due to alarm we go to bed after watching TV mobile.

We are travelling by bus train to the whole world. We can communicate to other people, entertain, we can connect to the whole world from a specific place, we can do all these things just because of science and technology, without science and technology life becomes painful hard in now a day. now scientist discovered the existence of life outside the Earth. this happens just because of science and technology which we have. now in future will have much more better technology to the compare of now.

Today science and technology have developed a lot. We can't spend life even a day without science and technology. Science and technology becomes our daily needs. Our body needs oxygen for living as same our life needs science and technology for living. We can't imagine life without science and technology.

We can go anywhere on the earth because of science and technology. Even we can go outside the Earth due to science and technology. scientist found the existence of life outside the earth or other planet with the help of science and technology. Science and technology comfort our life.

If we talk about only technology we have many technology right now. Also we have advanced technology for make life easy of human beings. Like our phone, a widely used device or commonly used device by almost all peoples. now a mobile phone plays an important role in our life, without mobile phone life becomes hard, extreme hard. now mobiles is using by millions of peoples.

we can communicate to other people which is far off distance from another people in just a second just because of science and technology. we can chat, talk face to face, video call just in a single click by mobile. actually science and technology improved our life.

we can save our life just because of science and technology. earth has limited number of natural resource which is very important to existence of life on Earth for human beings. now due to population and many other stuff natural resource shot down. so it will be difficult to exist on earth but we have advanced science and advanced technology to fulfill this defect, but we have worry a little about. we have to save natural resource.

essay on science and technology in 300 words

The 21st century is going to be the era of science and technology. The invention which has completely changed the life-style of the people. In this modern day of computer, the computer has, in recent years, triggered a new phase of development of mankind. the potentials of the computer are so vast.

The 20th century was totally dependent on computers and the list of the functions which computer performs for man includes business transactions, education, communications and like is endless. In this age of science and technology, when the technology revolution has turned the world into a global village. Today communication is power, communication is money, fun, entertainment and intelligence.

communication satellites have also made a significant contribution towards the development of communication network. Recently a global communication giant which has a constellation of 65 satellites, has launched its global mobile personal calling service(GMPCS) all over the world including India just because of science and technology.

The present age is the age of science and technologies. with the introduction of new technologies, the dimensions of communication system will also change and the time is not far when people will be putting through their calls from the Moon and other planets as if they wil speaking from the next room.

Today, we are simply overwhelmed by the vast possibilities of new technologies, a whole new range of user-friendly computers, optic fibre, ISDN, Computer graphics, CD-ROMS, MDTV and many more.

the result of technology revolution is that all the future business will be online.This development has lead to the growth of new concept called e-commerce. With the simple push of a button the entire shoppers list will be appear on the screen from where they can order the products of their choice. This is not possible without science and technology.

Science and technology essay in 800 words

Science and technology has changed our life. Technology is not possible without science. We can't imagine how hard our life would be without science. Now a day we are totally dependent on technology. But technology has its own advantage and disadvantage. We can't ignore them.

But we will today discuss about advantage of science and technology.

The biggest advantage of science and technology are it gives us computer and electricity .

Computer and electricity and one of the major inventions by human beings. So in this age of science and technology there will be less if we talk about computer and electricity. But still we will discuss about computer and electricity in more detail.

Computer is an electronic processing machine. It works more or less like the human brain and brings forth results at a marvellous speed. It has an era of automation. the basic feature of a computer is that it performs logical operations on inputs and yields answer according to programmed instruction during the last two decades of 20th century, the world seems to have undergone a computer revolution in which information processing and tribals is being done at an incredible speed.

Charles Babbage was the first man to think of a machine which could stored and produced logarithmic tables way back in the mid-nineteenth century. Today, computer has become the cornerstone of our industrial growth. it has not only helped in increasing industrial production but the internet and information Highway has also helped in the percolation and transmission of information to peoples rooms. robots are being used in the study of active volcanoes in oceanography and in space research areas where provide inhospitable climates for human entry.

But is computer a boon or a bane? open Mansa divided on this question computers might replace human in certain specific areas. Computers will be specific to those areas in which progress has been hampered by the limitations of the human body. Computers might solve humanity's most pressing problems like energy crisis, machines programmed to work in AIDs, cancer research, etc. And might arrived at answers which are at present imperceivable to us.

Computer is no doubt a great creation. But we should also remember that "human existence is based upon two pillars compassion and knowledge. Compassion without knowledge is ineffective and knowledge without compassion is in human". the thought process going on within the protoplasmic computer in our skulls will not stop here, bird continue to produce things that would enhance human capabilities and make man's life on earth better and happier.

Electricity is one of the modern age. it is used for doing many things. In cities we have electric light. the switch is moved and the whole town becomes lighted.

there is a power-house for supplying electricity. the power-house generates electricity which is sent to different places through wires. Now, villagers are also having electric light. electricity is used not only for producing light but also for many other purposes.

Lamps and tapers have lost their importance. In there places men use electric light. we have now electric fans, electric lifts etc. In cities like Kolkata and Delhi there are electric tramp-car. In many countries trains run with the help of electricity. wireless works with electricity. mills required engines which work with electricity. It helps in printing papers and sending news. it is used for cooking foods and for curing diseases. Hydroelectricity has been discovered which can pump water from rivers to irrigate fields.

The government of India is working on many rivers projects. If success is achieved, people will drive great benefit. but atomic energy is more powerful than electricity.

electricity has got its dark side also. it has made life artificial. it has brought unemployment. electric currents often destroyed human life.

It appears that man will depends upon electricity for everything. If that really happens, men will become a machine and life will have no future.

Disadvantage of science and technology

it has made life artificial

it has brought unemployment

electric currents often destroyed human life

man will depends upon electricity for everything

men will become a machine and life will have no future

Essay on science and technology in 1000 words

Science and technology both plays a vital role in our life. Even in our day to day life. Our environment covered with science and technology. Now, a day human totally dependent on technology. The biggest reason behind this dependency is comfort and ease. Technology makes our life easier and comfortable. For example, Before 10 to 15 years ago there were no any tele communication or communicational devices like phone, mobile etc. At previous time people waited for letter, even a week or month. But Now, at the era of technology talking and communication becomes easier.

Science and technology are the endless topics. There will be no any limit to talk about. But we will try to short these topics as possible as quickly. we will covering all the latest information regarding science and technology. This essay on science and technology is also usable for SSC CHSL, UPSC exam.

We cannot imagine our life without science and technology. Everyday it gets just expand and expand. Because every day new technology are coming and old expired. This process will last forever, because of the presence of science in our life and this universe. If we compare between science and technology then science will be the winner. Because without science, technology not possible.

How much science and technology affect our life. If shows by our behaviour. We wake up in the morning with our phone and go to bed with same. Actually science and technology are fully controls us. Don't angry! This is the fact. But that's not mean that science and technology are always bad for us. Sometimes it helps us more, Sometimes it makes our life easier. But this is also the fact that it destroyed our youth. Now a day, children loves more to play games on phone, not in field. Due to this the health affected. Even study affected. And the important thing children didn't enjoy their childhood.

Science and technology cuts our social life. In this social networking era. There are many social networking sites like facebook, instagram etc has destroyed our man to man connection. We totally depend on science and technology. Even our work, education and many other things shifted on technology. This is the reason we all uses phone, checking emails, important notifications etc, while eating. This is the disadvantage of science and technology.

Science and technology helps our country in development sector. Basically in the field of industries. India is now at growing stage in industrial field. Even it may be small scale industries or any big industries. It is growing by leaps and bounds.

Science and technology have opened the door of space. Due to science and technology we can established future in other planet. The discovery of new planet and other information in space is just because of science and technology.

Science and technology also helps in the field of agriculture. In the improvement of our agricultural sector. There is a huge role of science and technology.

There are many advantages and disadvantages of science and technology. The first advantage of science and technology is, It makes our life more comfortable. The disadvantage of science and technology is, It makes us lazy and inactive. The second advantage of science and technology is, It saves our more time and work. But the disadvantage of science and technology is, It reduces human patient and hard work. The third advantage of science and technology is, It gives us electricity, communication, transport, computer, and many other things. But the disadvantage of all this things is, once sources over and there will no any electricity generator fuel then human faces lots of problems. And the last things of disadvantage of science and technology is, It pollute our earth's atmosphere.

9 798887 334769

Printed by Libri Plureos GmbH in Hamburg, Germany